FTCE
Reading K–12

This page intentionally left blank.

FTCE
Reading K–12

Kathleen Jasper, Ed.D.

NavaED
10600 Chevrolet Way #107
Estero, FL 33928

FTCE Reading K-12

Content Editors:
Jeremy Jasper
Jelena Vuksanovic

Designer:
Jennifer Edwards

Printed in the United States of America
ISBN: 9798615431722

Want more help?

Visit our **YouTube channel** and follow us on **Instagram** and **Twitter**. On YouTube, you'll find lots of videos about all things FTCE, and we provide additional tips, tricks, and discounts on our other social media accounts. Search NavaED to find us and follow us.

Visit our **Facebook Page**. Join us every Tuesday at 5 P.M. EST on our Facebook page for our live Facebook live math help. https://www.facebook.com/NavaEDFL/

Check out our **webinars**. You can purchase previous webinars on our website or watch for new live webinars to be announced. We are always searching for ways to provide you with the tools you need to be successful on your certification exams.

Visit our **website**. Check out our online course for the FTCE Professional Education Test. The online course includes all the information in the book as well as full worked out video explanations of each of the practice tests. https://navaed.com

Need technical assistance or have a question?
Email us at info@navaed.com

You've got this!

This page intentionally left blank.

Table of Contents

COMPETENCY 5 KNOWLEDGE OF ORAL AND WRITTEN LANGUAGE ACQUISITION AND BEGINNING READING

COMPETENCY 6 KNOWLEDGE OF ORAL AND WRITTEN LANGUAGE ACQUISITION AND BEGINNING READING

COMPETENCY 7 KNOWLEDGE OF ORAL AND WRITTEN LANGUAGE ACQUISITION AND BEGINNING READING

COMPETENCY 8 KNOWLEDGE OF READING FLUENCY AND READING COMPREHENSION

This page intentionally left blank.

How to Use this Book

Congratulations on your choice to become an educator. At NavaED, we value the importance and necessity of great educators; without you, many children's futures would be at risk. Nothing can replace enthusiastic, well-prepared teachers who love their subject area, love learning, and want to pass their knowledge and passion onto others. Our goal at NavaED is to make your transition into a position in education as smooth as possible when it comes to certification exams and beyond.

How to Study

It is our recommendation that you really take the time to read through the entire book. The writers at NavaED have worked as teachers, school level administrators, and district level administrators, so we have experienced certification tests first hand. We know what is expected of teachers and administrators from the school level, the district level, and the state level-because we've been there ourselves. We have used this knowledge to break down and weed through all the information provided about certification tests so that we could prepare a comprehensive study guide that will give you the tools, tips, and resources to be successful on your certification exam.

If you only have a short amount of time to prepare for your exam, take the practice test at the end of the book. Use the answer explanations provided to determine what competencies you may still need to master, and read through those sections of the book. After reading through specific competencies, work through the competency's additional practice problems at the end to re-test your mastery of the material. If time allows, work through the remaining practice test.

Tips, Tricks, and Strategies

We've worked hundreds of hours studying the test blueprints and test items to provide you with strategies and tips for navigating questions and concepts on the FTCE Reading K-12 Test.

Remember, we've been there, and we can verify our strategies work and our tips are valid. Our materials are designed to get you through all the skills on this test.

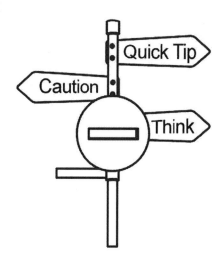

Education has its own specific set of terms, lingo, and buzz words educators use throughout their careers. These phrases and acronyms are well-known to many who are already teachers and administrators. However, for those just entering the profession, this education language can be confusing. To help you get the most out of this book, we have defined the words and phrases ubiquitous to this exam and to the profession (we call them *Good Words*). Understanding these education buzz words will help you locate correct answer choices on the exam. Chances are, if there is an education buzz word in an answer choice, it is probably the correct answer.

Throughout the book, we highlight various tips and strategies. We've broken them down into four categories and identify them with icons. Use the guide that follows to help you understand each type of tip we provide.

QUICK TIPS: These tips are represented with a megaphone and are strategies that will help you answer questions on the FTCE Reading K-12 Test. Tips may include vocabulary you need to know or strategies for answering questions for a particular skill or competency.

 TEST TIPS: Test tips are represented with a light bulb and are specific tips that you need to know about taking the test. These tips point out specific test taking strategies that can be, and should be, used while taking the FTCE Reading K-12 Test.

 THINK ABOUT IT: These tips are scenario-based teaching tips that are sound educational practices. These tips are not necessarily tested concepts, but they provide background information to help make sense of concepts and give necessary information to help answer questions on the FTCE Reading K-12 Test.

 CAUTION: Caution tips are specific pitfalls to watch out for when selecting your answer choice on the FTCE Reading K-12 . Test writers are very good at creating distracting answer choices that seem like good options. We show you what to watch for when it comes to distractors, so you avoid these pitfalls.

Good Words

Throughout this publication, we will direct your attention to words or phrases we call *good words*. Identifying good words in the answer choices before even reading the question is a NavaED test taking strategy. What we call good words come from the Florida Educator Accomplish Practices (FEAPs); these words and phrases are also discussed in the test specifications and blueprints for the Florida Teacher Certification Exams. You will often find good words in the correct answer choices, so be on the lookout for these when taking the exam. We will highlight good words throughout the text. A comprehensive list starts on page 151.

Book Organization

The sections of this book are arranged by competency, just like the FTCE Reading K-12 Test. Each competency is its own section, so that if you only need to concentrate on a specific competency, you can do so without having to weed out other sections and information. In addition, each competency is broken down by skills. Within each of the skill sections are examples and explanations of what you need to know to be successful on the FTCE Reading K-12 Test.

Competency Practice Problems

At the end of each competency we include 10 additional practice problems. These are problems on top of the 120-question practice test and additional examples throughout the book. Use these extra practice problems to determine if you have a firm grasp on each of the competencies. If you do not get at least 7 of the extra practice problems correct, revisit the competency.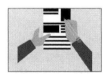

Practice Test

There is a 120-question practice test in this book. We break our practice test down by competency in the solutions so that you can focus on each competency, if needed. We suggest that before starting a competency, complete the practice test to determine where your strengths and weaknesses lie. Then, after reading and working through all the competencies and extra practice problems, retake the practice test. Mark areas that may still need improvement, go back and study those skills.

About the Test

TEST FORMAT

The FTCE Reading K-12 Test is a computer-based multiple choice test with 120 questions. You will have 2 hours and 30 minutes to complete the test. The skills on the FTCE Reading K-12 Test are aligned to the Florida's reading standards. Most questions on this test will be scenario based.

TEST REGISTRATION

To register for any FTCE/FELE test, you must have an FTCE/FELE account. To create or login to your account, access the website http://www.fl.nesinc.com/.

When registering for an account, you have to select a test you want to take, answer background questions, and agree to testing policies. Make sure to read through all the testing policies so that you know what to expect.

Once registered, you can schedule a test. You will have to select the testing location, date, and time. You will also be expected to pay for your test at this time, and you can choose to have your scores sent to a particular institution. Sending your scores to an institution is suggested. Even if you do not pass the test, it shows that you are working towards your required certification. It is not uncommon to not pass a certification test on your first try. Do not worry that the district or your school will judge you; they'd rather know that you are working toward certification rather than it appear you are not making any attempt at all.

Once your test is scheduled, you will receive an email from the testing center that outlines their guidelines. **Read this email carefully**. The email will include the testing location, test you are taking, the time of the scheduled test, what you can bring, test taking policies, where to access practice materials, and arrival time. **The arrival time is NOT the same as the test time**. They have the right to cancel your test if you do not show up at the arrival time.

WHAT TO EXPECT ON TEST DAY

When you arrive at the testing center, be prepared to tell the check-in person the test you are taking and present them your picture ID. You may be required to read over the testing center rules again and sign off that you have read and accept their rules.

The testing center will have lockers for you to store your personal items. ALL the personal items you bring with you except for glasses and a jacket must be placed in a locker.

Things you should not wear or bring include:
- writing utensils
- scratch paper
- cheat sheets
- sunglasses
- necklaces and bracelets
- headphones
- snacks and drinks
- electronics, such as a fitbit, smart watch, cell phone, or any handheld device

If you bring a wallet, purse, cell phone, keys or other item not allowed into the testing room or wear jewelry that is not permitted, you will have to store these items in a locker until your test is complete. You are not able to access these items during the test for test security reasons.

If you wear glasses, the glasses will be checked to ensure they do not have any recording devices on them. You may also be asked to have a finger or palm scan, you may be asked to empty your pockets, and you may be scanned with a handheld wand by security personnel. Each testing center is a little different, so be prepared for any of these things. They take test security very seriously at testing centers.

DURING THE TEST

You are allowed breaks during a test. All breaks must be taken outside of the exam room. You cannot get up and stretch or walk around the testing room during a break because of the disruption it may cause to other test takers. Test centers administer all types of exams for all different job types, so do not assume that everyone there is taking the same test that you are.

There are two types of breaks, scheduled breaks and unscheduled breaks. A *scheduled break* is part of the test. There are instructions on the testing screen if you are given a scheduled break. These breaks do NOT count against your testing time and are usually given during longer exams.

An *unscheduled break* is one that you elect to take. This includes if you have to use the restroom during your test. During an unscheduled break, your testing clock is not paused, meaning this break counts against your time. We strongly suggest you use the restroom right before entering the test.

Every test is different, so if you are taking more than one test, do not assume the same break rules apply. Always read the information sent to you about your test.

MATERIALS PROVIDED

For the FTCE Reading K-12 Test, the following items are provided:
- dry erase grid paper in a spiral notebook
- dry erase marker
- noise canceling headphones

You are allowed to bring earplugs if noise bothers you during testing. The noise canceling headphones that are provided block out some, but not all noise. Some test takers may be taking a test that requires a lot of typing, and some people are very loud typers. Constant click-clacking on the keyboard may distract you from being able to concentrate. There may also be unavoidable outdoor noises, such as building maintenance or construction taking place, which may cause you to be distracted.

AFTER TESTING

Once your test is complete, a proctor will come make sure your test is submitted and usher you from the testing area. Because the test is a multiple choice test, you may receive an unofficial score report letting you know if you passed or failed. If you are down to the wire with this test requirement, your district will probably accept this report as temporary proof that you have passed the FTCE Professional Education Test. If you do not receive an unofficial score report, this does not mean you failed. It simply means they have reformatted some questions on the test and are trying out this new format. In this case, they do not release scores on site.

All test scores will be sent to your FTCE/FELE account that you created when you signed up for the test. Check this site regularly for your official score reports. If you do not pass the test, your score report will include a breakdown by competency to let you know how many points the competency was worth and how many points you earned.

Overview | FTCE Reading K–12 Test

The Florida Teacher Certification Examinations (FTCE) are developed and produced by the Florida Department of Education. The content on the FTCE Professional Education Test was identified and validated by a committee of education specialists, all from Florida. The material on the test is aligned to the Florida Educator Accomplished Practices.

Test at a Glance	
Test Name	FTCE Reading K–12 Test
Format	Computer-based test (CBT)
Time	2 hours and 30 minutes; about 1 minute 15 seconds per question
Number of Questions	Approximately 120; all multiple choice (A, B, C, D)
Passing Score	A scaled score of at least 200; Approximately 71% of the questions correct or 84 out of 120 questions correct; You can miss approximately 36 questions and still pass.
Items Provided	Dry erase spiral-bound notepad and marker

	Competency	Approximate % of total questions	Approximate # of total questions
1.	Knowledge of research and theories of reading processes	10%	12
2.	Knowledge of text types and structures	10%	12
3.	Knowledge of reading assessment and evaluation	10%	12
4.	Knowledge of learning environments and procedures that support reading	10%	12
5.	Knowledge of oral and written language acquisition and beginning reading	11%	13
6.	Knowledge of phonics and word recognition	12%	14-15
7.	Knowledge of vocabulary acquisition and use	12%	14-15
8.	Knowledge of reading fluency and reading comprehension	15%	18
9.	Knowledge of reading program development, implementation, and coordination	10%	12

This page intentionally left blank.

Competency 1 | Knowledge of research and theories of reading processes

1. Identify characteristics and sources of valid reading research.

2. Identify foundational theorists and differentiate among theories of reading processes and development.

3. Relate instructional applications to theories of reading processes and development.

1. Identify characteristics and sources of valid reading research.

As a reading teacher, it is important that you stay well-informed about the pedagogy and practice of teaching reading. Educators are consistently publishing relevant research that governs the profession. Teachers must continually seek out valid and reliable research so they can make informed and appropriate decisions in the classroom.

Questions to ask when evaluating research:

1. **Is the research reliable and valid?**

   - **Validity** refers to how sound the research is in both the design and methods. Validity is the extent to which the findings in the study represent the phenomenon measured in the study.

     - **Internal Validity** refers to how well a study is conducted.

     - **External Validity** refers to how applicable the findings are to the real world.

   - **Reliability** refers to the degree of consistency in the measure. A study is considered reliable when it yields similar results under similar conditions after being conducted repeatedly.

2. **Are the authors authorities or experts in their fields?** Authors who are prolific in their space tend to produce reliable and valid research. Be sure to check the author(s).

3. **Is the research current?** Using research conducted in the last 3 years is more effective than using research from the last 20 years. That doesn't mean that past studies are not important. Plenty of the early research in reading is considered seminal. But when looking for trends in reading and new ways to teach, using current research is best.

4. **Is the research scholarly?** Teachers should consider research that comes from peer-reviewed academic journals. Websites and blogs often contain valid and reliable research. However, to be sure that the research is legitimate, go straight to the academic journal where it was published. Be sure to check the bibliography in the study.

5. **Is the research objective?** Research should be unbiased and objective; it should address questions without opinions or agenda. Often, private companies that sell reading programs will publish research. It is important that teachers differentiate between objective research and research that is skewed one way. You can do this by looking at several studies about a topic. Look for trends and consistencies between and among the studies.

6. **Is the research relevant to the profession?** There are a lot of studies out there with important information. You should be seeking out research in the areas that fit your particular job. For example, if you are a reading teacher in a school with a large population of English language learners, you should seek out research relevant to that area.

(University of Massachusetts Boston, 2019)

2. **Identify foundational theorists and differentiate among theories of reading processes and development.**

On the FTCE Reading K-12 exam, you will be asked to identify influential reading theorists and the foundational theories that govern reading. In most cases, these questions will be presented in scenarios, and you will be required to identify the theorist or theory that aligns with the scenario.

MAIN READING THEORISTS

▶ B.F. Skinner, Edward Thorndike, and John Watson

These three theorists are behaviorists and believed learning is a function of change in overt behavior. Changes in behavior are the result of an individual's response to events (stimuli) that occur in the environment. A reinforcer is anything that strengthens the desired response. It could be verbal praise, a good grade or a feeling of increased accomplishment or satisfaction. External rewards and motivations are often associated with behaviorism.

TEST TIP:

Behaviorist strategies or external rewards, such as pizza parties, extra time in the library, and accolades, are typically not the correct answer on this exam when it comes to motivation. Motivation for reading should come from intrinsic value.

▶ Jean Piaget

Piaget is widely known for his stages of cognitive development. This is a framework for how students develop intellectually through various stages. Piaget (1972) asserted that cognitive development was a reorganization of mental processes resulting from biological maturation and environmental experience.

Piaget's 4 Stages of Cognitive Development		
Sensorimotor	0–2 years	Children at this stage figure out the world through sensory and motor experiences. Object permanence and separation anxiety are hallmarks of this stage.
Pre-operational	2–6 years	Children at this stage identify and use symbols for objects but do not have the ability to apply logical reasoning. They know how to play pretend and are egocentric.
Concrete operational	7–12 years	Logical reasoning about concrete objects kicks in during this stage. Conservation, reversibility, serial ordering, and understanding cause and effect relationships are hallmarks of this stage, but thinking is still limited to the concrete.
Formal operational	12 years–adult	Abstract thinking such as logic, deductive reasoning, comparison, and classification are demonstrated by the individual in this stage.

(Piaget, 1972)

▶ Lev Vygotsky

Vygotsky's theories stress the fundamental role of social interaction in the development of cognition. He believed strongly that community plays a central role in the process of making meaning. Vygotsky is most widely known for the Zone of Proximal Development (ZPD), which he asserted is the distance between the actual developmental level as determined by independent problem solving and the level of potential development as determined through problem-solving under adult guidance, or in collaboration with more capable peers (Vygotsky, 1978). Helping someone move through the Zone of Proximal Development depends on 3 core aspects:

1. The presence of someone with knowledge and skills beyond that of the learner (a more knowledgeable other).

2. Social interactions with a skillful tutor that allow the learner to observe and practice their skills.

3. Scaffolding, or supportive activities provided by the educator, or more competent peer, to support the student as he or she is led through the ZPD.

▶ Frank Smith (Whole Language)

Frank Smith's theory of whole language is the opposite of the traditional methods of teaching reading. Whole language encourages students to pursue "authentic" reading and writing. Frank Smith advocates skills instruction and programmed mastery learning behavioristic schemes be replaced with reading and writing assignments that are meaningful for each dynamic individual. Students come to English classes with an intrinsic desire to make sense of their world and to do so through communication. Whole language teachers acknowledge this linguistic skill and motivation and design their classes so that learning in school is consonant with the inventive spirit and personal goals of each student (Shafer, 1998).

▶ Louise Rosenblatt

Louise Rosenblatt's theories are grounded in constructivism—learning is constructed through authentic, real-world experiences. The act of reading literature involves a transaction between the reader and the text. Reading response journals and relating text to self are two activities that align with this theory.

▶ Noam Chomsky

Noam Chomsky's reading theory asserts that humans have an instinct or an innate sense of language and literacy. He dubbed this instinct *universal grammar*—language is basic instinct.

---

3. Relate instructional applications to theories of reading processes and development.

This part of the exam will require you to identify what theories are being applied in a classroom situation. You will most likely be given a classroom scenario, and you will be required to choose the theorist or theory the situation represents.

Reading approaches are typically categorized by theories, approaches, and theorists. Think of the theories as evolutions in reading instruction. Therefore, behaviorism is traditional, and transnationalism is modern.

	Theory	Theorist	Practice	Application to Reading
Behaviorism	Traditional	Skinner Thorndike Watson	Reading is developed by habit formation, brought about by the repeated association of a stimulus with a response (Omaggio, 1993)	Bottom Up – Reading is a linear process and the focus should be on phonics.
Cognitivism	Traditional/Modern	Piaget	Reading is developed by connecting information in the text with the knowledge the reader brings to the act of reading.	Top Down – Building schema and using background knowledge is essential to developing reading.
Constructivism	Modern	Louise Rosenblatt	Using before reading, during reading, and after reading techniques to organize understanding of text	Metacognitive (thinking about thinking) – Thinking about what the brain does when going through the process of reading is essential in building reading skills.

IN THE CLASSROOM

► **Vygotsky (Zone of Proximal Development)**

Cooperative learning is usually associated with Vygotsky because he believed learning takes place in social situations. Scaffolding is also a big part of Vygotsky's approach to learning.

- Students are working in literature circles to read and analyze text.
- The teacher is showing students how to read the text. Then they read together. Then the student reads on her own. This is the **I do, we do, you do** (gradual release) method.

▶ Piaget (Stages of Cognitive Development)

Students build schema as they move through the stages of cognitive development.

- Students are discussing what they already know about rocks before reading a passage on different types of rocks.

- A teacher is activating students' background knowledge by using a KWL[1] chart.

K	W	L
What do I already know?	What do I want to learn?	What did I learn?
Cells are small.	What do cells do?	Parts of the cell and how they interact to support life

Whole language is a theory derived from the constructivist view that language should be learned not as isolated skills but rather an integration of skills applied to authentic reading and writing tasks.

QUICK TIP:

The theory of constructivism is present throughout the FTCE Reading K-12 Test. Constructivism is a holistic philosophy that supports the idea that learning and problem solving should reflect real-life contexts where the environment is very rich in information and there are no right answers (embedded knowledge). Learning should include authentic tasks. Keep this in mind when answering questions, especially scenario questions. Look for answers that align with the philosophy of constructivism.

---

1   A KWL table, or KWL chart, is a graphic organizer designed to help build prior knowledge and guide learning. The letters KWL are an acronym for what students in the course of a lesson already know (K-prior knowledge), what they want to know (W), and what they ultimately learn (L).

This page intentionally left blank.

1. A teacher strongly believes that reading is innate and that students have an instinct to understand language. The teacher's views mostly align with which reading theorist?

    A. Louise Rosenblatt

    B. Noam Chomsky

    C. Jean Piaget

    D. Lev Vygotsky

2. A teacher is reading over recent research about cooperative learning in reading. She wants to apply research-based strategies outlined in the study in her classroom instruction. What should she be sure to consider before implementing these methods?

    A. Is the author reputable?

    B. Is the study published on the internet?

    C. Is the study reliable and valid?

    D. Have others in her field read the study?

3. The reading theory that focuses on phonics instruction is:

    A. Metacognition

    B. Constructivism

    C. Top down

    D. Bottom up

4. Which of the following practices aligns with the theory of cognitive development outlined by Jean Piaget?

    A. Students are filling out a KWL chart to activate prior knowledge or schema.

    B. Students are reading in groups to understand text together.

    C. Students are focusing on phonics applications in words.

    D. Students are working in whole language centers.

5. Where is the best place for a teacher to obtain the most relevant, reliable, and valid research in the area of reading instruction?

    A. A peer-reviewed academic journal

    B. A reputable reading company's website

    C. A university website

    D. The district's reading resource center

6. What is it called when a study's findings can be applied to real-world situations?

    A. Internal validity

    B. External validity

    C. Accuracy

    D. Reliability

7. Students often learn new knowledge that contradicts their previous knowledge. Which of the following theories describes this phenomenon?

    A. Schema theory

    B. Social constructivism

    C. Cognitive dissonance

    D. Zone of Proximal Development

8. The quality of getting consistent results on an assessment is known as:

    A. Internal validity

    B. External validity

    C. Formative assessment

    D. Reliability

9. Mrs. Smith believes that her role as a teacher is to facilitate learning. Students in her class work in groups, create projects, and reflect on the successes and failures. Which of the following theories aligns with Mrs. Smith's philosophy?

    A. Zone of Proximal Development

    B. Schema theory

    C. Scaffolding

    D. Social Constructivism

10. Frank Smith advocates skills instruction and programmed mastery learning behavioristic schemes be replaced with reading and writing assignments that are meaningful for each dynamic individual. This is called:

    A. Phonics approach

    B. Phonemic Awareness approach

    C. Whole Language approach

    D. Schema approach

Competency 1 | Practice Problems Answer Explanations

Number	Answer	Explanation
1.	B	Noam Chomsky believed that humans have an instinct to read. He called this Universal Grammar. Louise Rosenblatt is a constructivist. Piaget believed in building schema or background knowledge for reading. Finally, Vygotsky's theories centered around the social aspect of learning to read.
2.	C	The most important thing to consider is whether or not the research is reliable and valid. Validity is the extent to which the findings in the study represent the phenomenon measured in the study. Reliability refers to the degree of consistency in the measure.
3.	D	Phonics instruction focuses on the linear process of reading. It is aligned with the bottom up theory of reading.
4.	A	Jean Piaget proposed that schema or background knowledge is essential in learning to read. Therefore, using a KWL chart to develop or activate background knowledge is the best answer here.
5.	A	While teachers can find research everywhere, a peer-reviewed academic journal is the best place to find relevant, reliable, and valid research.
6.	B	**Internal Validity** – The student was conducted properly and results can be applied *within* the context of the study. **External Validity** - Results can be generalized to the *outside* world. **Accuracy** – Precision of results (nonsense answer for this problem) **Reliability** - The consistency of the measure. (Results are consistent when the test is administered again and again).
7.	A	Schema is related to prior knowledge. Therefore, A is the best answer.
8.	D	**Reliability** - The consistency of the measure. (Results are consistent when the test is administered again and again).
9.	D	Constructivism is a holistic philosophy that supports the idea that learning and problem solving should reflect real-life contexts where the environment is very rich in information and there are no right answers (embedded knowledge). Learning should include authentic tasks.
10.	C	Whole language is a theory derived from the constructivist view that language should be learned not as isolated skills but rather an integration of skills applied to authentic reading and writing tasks.

This page intentionally left blank.

Competency 2 | Knowledge of text types and structures

1. Identify text structures and text features of literary and informational texts.

2. Differentiate among the characteristics, features, and elements of various literary and informational genres and formats of texts for reading and writing.

3. Evaluate and select appropriate texts to reflect and support the backgrounds of diverse learners while matching texts to student interest.

4. Determine criteria for evaluating and selecting both print and nonprint texts for instructional use.

5. Evaluate and select texts at appropriate reading levels and text complexity for diverse learners.

1. Identify text structures and text features of literary and informational texts.

Understanding structural elements of text can positively impact students' literacy skills. When students understand the structure of text, they can construct, examine, and extend the meaning in text, which leads to a depth of understanding of the text.

Text structure refers to how the information is organized in the text and can help students identify the following elements of the text.

Main idea and details – The story or passage has an overarching viewpoint or idea and then supports that idea with details throughout the text.

Compare and contrast – The story or text finds similarities and differences between and among people, places and situations.

Chronological – The story or passage goes in order by time.

Cause and effect – The story or passage presents something that happens and then the result or effect of an action.

Problem/Solution – The story or passage presents a problem and then possible solutions to the problem.

Inferences – A conclusion based on evidence and reasoning. A logical "guess" based on something that is happening in the story.

Key details – Words or phrases that help the reader answer questions about the text. Key details give information by asking questions like who, what, where, when, and why.

On the exam, you will be given a short excerpt of text, and you will be expected to identify the type text structure used on the passage. The following is an example of how this would look on the exam.

Example 1 Text structure

Use the following excerpt to answer the question.

Many Americans are in debt because of student loans. Because of predatory lending practices and the high price of higher education, students were compelled to borrow money for college. Now many Americans cannot buy homes or invest in their retirement because they are paying off student debt.

The excerpt is an example of:

A. Problem/solution

B. Compare and contrast

C. Main idea and details

D. Cause and effect

SOLUTION

The passage is outlining the cause—predatory lending practices and high cost for higher education—and the effect—Americans are in debt and cannot afford to buy houses or save for retirement.

Correct Answer: D

Point of View

Understanding the **author's point of view** will help with comprehension of the text. The following table outlines different points of view used in text.

Narrative	Definition
First Person	A narrator in the story recounts his or her own perspective, experience or impressions. The pronouns *I, we, me, us*, are used in the text.
Second Person	The story is written in the perspective of *you*.
Third Person Objective	The narrator remains a detached observer, telling only the stories action and dialogue.
Third Person Limited	The narrator tells the story from the viewpoint of one character in the story.
Third Person Omniscient	The narrator has unlimited knowledge and can describe every characters' thoughts and interpret their behaviors. Omniscient means all-knowing

*Third person narrative is often used in informational text because it is the most objective point of view.

2. **Differentiate among the characteristics, features, and elements of various literary and informational genres and formats of texts for reading and writing.**

Using a balanced literary approach is key when teaching students how to read. Teachers can use various types of literature to implement a balanced literacy program in the classroom. A balanced literacy program uses a combination of informational and literary texts.

Text Type	Examples
Informational Text	Written primarily to inform
	Literary nonfiction
	History/social science texts
	Science/technical texts
	Digital texts
Literary Text	Adventure
	Folktales
	Legends
	Fables
	Fantasy
	Realistic fiction
	Myths

It is also imperative that teachers expose students to a variety of genres for reading and writing.

Genres are categories of artistic composition characterized by similarities in form, style, or subject matter. The main genres recognized in English language arts instruction are fiction, nonfiction, poetry, and drama. Subgenres are particular categories within a genre. For example, historical fiction is a subgenre of fiction. See the following table for examples of different genres.

Genre of Writing	Subgenre
Fiction	**Realistic fiction** – Fictional stories that could be true. **Historical fiction** – Fictional stories set during a real event or time in history. These stories will have historically accurate events and locations. **Science fiction** – Fictional stories that focus on space, the future, aliens, and other galaxies. **Fantasy** – Fictional stories that include monsters, fairies, magic, and/or other fantastical elements.
Nonfiction	**Informational text** – Text that informs the reader, such as a social science textbook or informational brochure. **Biographies** – Text that tells the life of another person. The author is not the person in the biography. **Autobiographies** – Text that describes one's own life. The author is the person in the autobiography. **Expository Nonfiction** – Text that informs the reader. The author is objective. **Narrative Nonfiction** – Text that presents a true story written in a style more closely associated with fiction.
Poetry	**Limerick** – A humorous verse of three long and two short lines rhyming (aabba). **Sonnet** – A poem of 14 lines using any of a number of formal rhyme schemes. **Epic** – A long narrative that focuses on the trials and tribulations of a hero or god-like character who represents the cultural values of a race, nation, or religious group. **Haiku** – A Japanese poem consisting of 3 lines and 17 syllables. Each line has a set number of syllables: line 1 has 5 syllables; line 2 has 7 syllables; line 3 has 5 syllables.
Folklore	**Fable** – A short story that includes animals who speak and act like humans. There is usually a moral at the end of a fable. **Myth** – A story that showcases gods or goddesses and typically outlines the creation of something. **Legend** – A story that may have once been true but is exaggerated, usually about extraordinary human beings. **Fairy tale** – A story that has both human and magical creatures in it.
Dramas	**Comedy** - Entertainment consisting of jokes and satirical sketches intended to make an audience laugh. **Tragedy** – A play dealing with tragic events and having an unhappy ending, especially concerning the downfall of the main character.

On the exam you will be given a title or an excerpt, and you will be required to identify the genre or subgenre of the text.

Example **1** **Genres**

A memoir is an example of:

    A. Narrative nonfiction

    B. Expository nonfiction

    C. Realistic fiction

    D. Historical fiction

SOLUTION

In a memoir, the author is writing about her own life and uses story-like elements. The text comes from the person's point of view, so it is not completely objective.

Correct Answer: A

3. **Evaluate and select appropriate texts to reflect and support the backgrounds of diverse learners while matching texts to student interest.**

Creating a classroom culture that supports the background of all students is a big part of the reading teacher's purpose. Reading teachers have the power to bring multicultural texts and stories to students. This can be a daunting task for new teachers because many things should be considered when selecting multicultural texts.

On the exam, you will be required to consider the following when answering questions about diversity in the classroom and choosing literature and text that represents all students.

Accuracy - Accuracy of cultural representation is a crucial aspect of high-quality, multicultural literature, and books must contain current, correct information to avoid reinforcing stereotypes (Agosto, 2002; Shioshita, 1997).

Authentic dialogue – The dialogue in the text should accurately represent culturally-specific oral traditions (Landt, 2006).

Presentation of information or issues – The information in the text should not leave out information that is unfavorable to the dominant culture.

On the exam, you will be required to identify proper practices and methods for choosing literature that supports and celebrates all cultures and that helps students see many perspectives.

Example **1** **Appropriate text selection**

Ms. Jones is preparing for a reading lesson using historical elements from WWII, specifically Japanese internment camps. What would be the most important approach for Ms. Jones to take when choosing literature and informational text for this lesson?

    A. Select text that is on students' reading level, so they don't struggle with complex concepts presented in the text.

    B. Evaluate whether the information in the literature and text accurately presents information and events during that time.

    C. Survey the students to determine what students already know about WWII and Japanese internment camps.

    D. Omit pieces of the text that may be too intense or sensitive for students.

SOLUTION

The most important thing for this teacher to do is be sure the information is accurately portrayed. That may mean that there are intense and sensitive issues presented. Accuracy and truthful information is most important here.

Correct Answer: B

4. **Determine criteria for evaluating and selecting both print and nonprint texts for instructional use.**

An important part of being a reading teacher is evaluating and selecting print and nonprint materials for instructional use.

The very first thing to consider when choosing materials for the reading classroom is whether the materials are aligned to the state adopted standards. Always consult the standards before planning instruction or choosing instructional materials. After that, there are several things to consider. The following was taken from the Urbandale School District (2019) and is a comprehensive outline that should be considered when choosing materials for the reading classroom.

- Instructional materials should support the educational philosophy, goals and objectives of the District and the objectives of the curricular offering in which the materials will be used.

- Instructional materials should be appropriate for the age, emotional and social development, and ability level of the students for whom the materials are selected.

- Instructional materials should be diverse with respect to levels of difficulty, reader appeal, and should present a variety of points of view.

- Instructional materials should meet high standards of quality in factual content and presentation.

- Instructional materials should have aesthetic, cultural, literary, or social value. The value and impact of any literary work will be judged as a whole, taking into account the author's intent rather than individual words, phrases or incidents.

- Instructional materials should foster respect for men, women, the disabled, and minority groups and should portray a variety of roles and lifestyles open to people in today's world. Instructional materials should foster respect for cultural diversity.

- Instructional materials should be designed to motivate students to examine their own attitudes and behaviors and to comprehend their own duties, responsibilities, rights and privileges as participating citizens in a pluralistic society.

- Instructional materials should encourage students to use higher order thinking skills and to become informed decision-makers, to exercise freedom of thought and to make independent judgments through examination and evaluation of relevant information, evidence and differing viewpoints.

Example **1** **Selecting instructional materials**

Mr. Rodriguez is deciding what material he will use in a lesson over the next 9 weeks. What should be the first thing he considers when choosing instructional material?

    A. Is the material interesting and engaging?

    B. Is the material aligned to the state adopted standards?

    C. Is the material developmentally appropriate for students?

    D. Is the material culturally responsive?

SOLUTION

While all of these considerations are very important, the standards should be the first thing the teacher considers. After alignment is determined, the other three questions should be considered.

Correct Answer: B

5. **Evaluate and select texts at appropriate reading levels and text complexity for diverse learners**

When developing a balanced literacy approach in the classroom, teachers must use several data points to measure text complexity. It is important for teachers to select appropriate text levels because classrooms consist of students with varying abilities.

Measures of Text Complexity	
Qualitative	This type of data *cannot* be quantified. Instead, this data often comes in the form of anecdotal responses or scenarios. **Example**: While a teacher is observing students as they read, she notices some students are struggling. She decides to intervene with a different text or targeted interventions.
Quantitative	Data that *can* be quantified. When analyzing this type of data, teachers often look over reading levels, words per min and other measures that can be represented as numbers. **Example**: A teacher uses students' correct words per min to determine the Lexile levels of subsequent books they will use.
Reader and Task	These are the reader variables (motivation, knowledge, and experience) and task variables (purpose and complexity generated by the task assigned and the question posed). These variables can be measured both qualitatively and quantitatively. **Example**: A teacher chooses books that students have expressed interest in. The teacher understands the students are more likely to engage in text they are motivated to read.

(Lapp, Moss, Grant, & Johnson, 2015)

Text-leveling systems allow teachers to implement reading strategies to meet the needs of students. Identifying the different levels in the classroom will allow the teacher to drive instruction, focus on areas of improvement, and enrich students' individual needs. This data should be used to make instructional decisions.

There are several types of leveling systems. The following table outlines text-leveling systems teachers can use in the classroom.

	Grade Level	Guided Reading	Lexile Level (CCSS)	DRA Level	Reading Level
Emergent	Kindergarten	A	BR	A-1	1
		B		2-3	2
		C		4	3-4
		D		6	5-6
Early	Grade 1	E	190L-530L	8	7-8
		F		10	9-10
		G		12	11-12
		H		14	13-14
		I		16	15-17
		J		18	18-20
Transitional	Grade 2	K	420L-650L	20	18-20
		L		24	
		M		28	
	Grade 3	N	520L-820L	30	
		O		34	
		P		38	
Fluent	Grade 4	Q	740L-940L	40	
		R			
		S			
	Grade 5	T	830L-1010L	50	
		U			
		V			
	Grade 6	W	925L-1070L	60	
		X			
		Y			
Proficient	Grade 7	Z	970L-1120L	70	
	Grade 8	Z	1010L-1185L	80	
	Grade 9-12	Z(+)	1050L-1385L		

This page intentionally left blank.

1. When teachers use a variety of literary and informational text and select books from different genres and subgenres, they are using:

    A. student interest to drive instruction.

    B. a balanced literacy approach in the classroom.

    C. district guidelines to plan lessons.

    D. text complexity to challenge students.

2. Which of the following should be considered when planning a reading unit?

    A. Standards alignment

    B. Student interest

    C. Student reading levels

    D. Text appropriateness

3. What should be considered when choosing multicultural literature in the reading classroom?

    A. Accuracy, authentic dialogue, presentation of issues

    B. Authentic dialogue, appropriateness, interest

    C. Parent consent, students' world views, appropriateness

    D. Interest, reading levels, appropriateness

4. Ms. Jenson is deciding what text to use in an upcoming lesson. She is evaluating number of words per page, reading levels, and student reading scores to guide her instructional decisions. Ms. Jenson is using what type of measure of text complexity?

    A. Reader and task

    B. Qualitative

    C. Quantitative

    D. Rubric

5. Read the excerpt below and answer the question that follows.

    When she was sixteen years old, she was elected class president. She would later use those skills when she was elected governor in 1988. During her time as governor, she helped to create jobs in the state. When she retired, she volunteered with local organizations.

    What type of text structure is used above?

    A. Cause and effect

    B. Problem solution

    C. Compare and contrast

    D. Chronological

6. The narrator is telling a story about the characters and is providing information about the characters' thoughts and behaviors. What viewpoint is the narrator using?

    A. Limited

    B. Omniscient

    C. First person

    D. Second person

7. Which of the following would be the most effective approach for a teacher to take who is teaching students from diverse backgrounds?

    A. Read stories about other countries.

    B. Read stories authored from the perspectives people of different cultures.

    C. Allow students to pick stories they want to read.

    D. Send home a parent survey to ask for permission to read diverse texts.

8. Read the following paragraph and determine the text structure.

    A powerful tornado appeared out of nowhere. It was a tri-state tornado with high winds going about 200 mph. The people in the town were terrified because they've never seen a tornado of that size. Over 200 homes were destroyed that day.

    A. Problem and solution

    B. Chronological and sequential

    C. Cause and effect

    D. Descriptive

9. A teacher is looking over reading levels from a recent online reading assessment. She has several students who are at the BR level. These students are:

    A. Proficient

    B. Fluent

    C. Transitional

    D. Emergent

10. If a teacher is considering students' understanding and interests when picking texts to read in class, the teacher is considering what type of measures?

    A. Qualitative

    B. Quantitative

    C. Reader and task

    D. Genre

Competency 2 | Practice Problems Answer Explanations

Number	Answer	Explanation
1.	B	A balanced literacy program includes informational and literary text. It also includes text from different genres and subgenres.
2.	A	If there is an option in the answer choices to choose the standards, that should be the first choice. All the other answer choices are important. However, standards is the FIRST thing to reference.
3.	A	According to the research on multicultural literature, accuracy, authentic dialogue, and the presentation of issues are the most important considerations. Parent consent is not a consideration. Students' world views and interest are important but are not part of the main considerations for selecting multicultural text for the classroom.
4.	C	These measures are quantitative because they involve numbers—reading levels are presented as numbers, scores are presented as numbers, and words per page are presented as numbers. They are all quantifiable.
5.	D	This excerpt is happening in chronological order. It starts with the main character in high school. Then it moves to when she was governor. Then it showcases her retirement. This is in sequential order in time; therefore, it is chronological order.
6.	B	In third-person omniscient, the narrator tells the story from character's point of view but includes the thoughts and motives of the character. First person tells it from the narrator's point of view (I). Second person tells the story from the readers point of view (you). Limited is a nonsense answer here.
7.	B	Teaching students from diverse backgrounds means being culturally responsive in the classroom. Answer B is the most effective way to be culturally responsive.
8.	C	This is an example of the tornado (cause) impacting a town and homes (effect). No solutions are discussed, which eliminates answer A. The passage is not in chronological order. Finally, while there is some description of the tornado, cause and effect structure fits better than description.
9.	D	BR is the lowest reading level. Therefore, these students are emergent. All the other answer choices are above the emergent level.
10.	C	Reader and task measure the reader variables (motivation, knowledge, and experience) and task variables (purpose and complexity generated by the task assigned and the question posed).

This page intentionally left blank.

Competency 3 | Knowledge of reading assessment and evaluation

1. Differentiate among characteristics of norm-referenced, criterion-referenced, and performance-based assessments used for screening, diagnosis, progress monitoring, and outcomes.

2. Evaluate and select appropriate oral and written assessment instruments and practices using continuous text for monitoring individual student progress.

3. Analyze and interpret data from multiple informal and formal reading and writing assessments to guide whole-group instruction.

4. Analyze and interpret student data from multiple informal and formal reading and writing assessments to differentiate instruction and develop individual student goals for diverse learners.

5. Identify characteristics of students at varying reading levels.

1. **Differentiate among characteristics of norm-referenced, criterion-referenced, and performance-based assessments used for screening, diagnosis, progress monitoring, and outcomes.**

Every Florida Teacher Certification Exam has a component that measures your ability to select the most appropriate assessment at the appropriate time to measure the appropriate skill. You will be required to understand different assessments. Remember, assessments should always be used to make instructional decisions.

Assessment Type	Definition	Example
Diagnostic	A pre-assessment providing instructors with information about students' prior knowledge, preconceptions, and misconceptions before beginning a learning activity	Before starting a reading unit on earth space science, a teacher gives a quick assessment to determine students' prior knowledge of concepts in the text. She uses this information to make instructional decisions moving forward.
Formative	A range of formal and informal assessments or checks conducted by the teacher before, during, and after the learning process in order to modify instruction	A teacher walks around the room checking on students as they read. She might also write anecdotal notes to review later to help her design further instruction.
Summative	This assessment focuses on the outcomes. It is frequently used to measure the effectiveness of a program, lesson, or strategy	A reading teacher gives a midterm exam at the end of the semester mastery of standards.
Performance-Based	This assessment measures students' ability to apply the skills and knowledge learned from a unit or units of study; the task challenges students to use their higher-order, critical thinking skills to create a product or complete a process (Chun, 2010).	After reading a text about the Civil War, students develop stories about different historical figures in the war. Students then perform these stories in front of the class and answer questions.

Assessment Type	Definition	Example
Criterion-Referenced	This assessment measures student performance against a fixed set of predetermined criteria or learning standards.	At the end of the spring semester, students take the Florida Standards Assessment. The state uses the scores for accountability measures.
Norm-Referenced (Percentile)	This assessment or evaluation yields an estimate of the position of the tested individual in a predefined population with respect to the trait being measured.	The NAEP is an exam given every few years for data purposes only to compare students' reading scores across the U.S.
Screening	Screening is used to place students in appropriate classrooms or grade level.	Students are typically screened throughout the year to determine at what level they are reading. Placement decisions are made based on the outcomes of the screening.

The following is a scenario outlining how to use these assessments in the classroom.

- Before a unit on Native American Poetry, Ms. Jones gives students a **diagnostic assessment** in the form of a survey. She wants to measure students' current understanding of Native American poetry, background knowledge or experiences with Native American poetry, and any preconceptions or misconceptions about Native American culture.

- After she looks over the surveys, she realizes that her students do not have very much background knowledge on Native American culture. Many of the students have a stereotypical view of Native Americans. She designs several lessons, using the state standards, to help students **build their background knowledge (schema)** of Native American culture. Once they have developed the appropriate amount of background knowledge, she and her students begin to read the poetry.

- As she moves through the poetry reading and lessons, she uses **formative assessments** to measure students' fluency and comprehension by observing students as they read. She writes anecdotal notes documenting her observations. She also evaluates students' writing assignments to measure comprehension. Based on these formative assessments, she moves students into appropriate groups and prescribes specific and targeted interventions for students who are struggling.

- Throughout the entire lesson, she **progress monitors**—incrementally measuring effectiveness of interventions and classroom approaches. She discusses these findings in her professional learning community (PLC). She continues to make instructional decisions based on her progress monitoring.

- When she comes to the end of the unit, she wants to measure the effectiveness of the strategies and instruction she administered in class. She has students complete a **summative assessment**. Based on the results of the assessment, she sees that 80% of her students gained mastery of the standards. She sees that 10% are just below mastery, and 10% need continued interventions.

- Finally, students have shown progress over the unit, and she wants to have them apply their critical thinking skills. She has students choose from 3 different **performance-based assessments**: write an essay, develop and perform a presentation, or conduct a podcast. For all three assessments, she has a specific rubric outlining the expectations of each one.

2. Evaluate and select appropriate oral and written assessment instruments and practices using continuous text for monitoring individual student progress.

The most widely used assessment is a multiple-choice assessment, also known as selected response. However, this type of assessment does not always provide the necessary data when it comes to assessing students' reading abilities and students' needs. Often, an oral assessment or written assessment is more effective than a traditional assessment.

ORAL ASSESSMENTS

In an oral assessment, students show what they know by communicating by word of mouth. In an oral assessment, students will often answer questions about a story—sequence, plot, characters, etc. Oral assessments can also be used to measure fluency. Oral assessments can be used before reading to measure prior knowledge, during reading to measure understanding, and after reading to measure overall comprehension.

Oral assessments are helpful when working with English Language Learners (ELLs). Often, ELLs will understand a story or passage but may be unable to communicate what they know in writing. If the teacher is trying to assess comprehension, ELLs can orally communicate what they have read. This ensures the teacher is assessing the correct skill—comprehension. If the teacher insists on written communication, the teacher is not assessing comprehension, but rather she is assessing English writing skills.

WRITTEN ASSESSMENTS

Written assessments are considered authentic assessments because they give a comprehensive view of what a student knows about a particular topic. Written assessments can be as simple as filling in the blank or as complex as writing an essay on a topic. Journals are often used in the reading classroom to allow students an outlet to express how they feel about a story or text.

3. Analyze and interpret data from multiple informal and formal reading and writing assessments to guide whole-group instruction.

Effective reading teachers use data to make instructional decisions. As a reading teacher, you will use lots of informal assessments—observations, quick checks, questioning techniques, journal entries, and more— to see how your students are developing their reading and writing skills. You will also use a variety of formal assessments like benchmark tests and state assessments to measure outcomes.

Remember, informal assessments are typically used to progress monitor. Formal assessments are typically used to measure outcomes. Both formal and informal assessments are used to make instructional decisions and to differentiate instruction based on each student's individual needs.

TYPES OF FORMAL READING AND WRITING ASSESSMENTS

Formal reading and writing assessments come in many varieties. Perhaps the most common type of formal reading and writing assessments are state standardized assessments (criterion-referenced). These exams assess students' mastery of the state standards. Formal reading and writing assessments usually fall under the category *summative assessments* because they are used to measure outcomes.

There are certain benchmarks students must achieve on formal assessments in order to be deemed proficient. Typically, these tests are timed. For formal reading assessments, students must read passages and answer comprehension questions. For formal writing assessments, students are given a writing prompt and must complete a coherent, organized, and comprehensible essay in a certain amount of time. The scores from these tests are often used to promote or retain students.

TYPES OF INFORMAL READING AND WRITING ASSESSMENTS

Not all assessments need to be formal. In fact, the data collected from informal assessments can be very beneficial to the teacher when making decisions. Remember, informal assessments are often associated with formative assessments. Typically, informal reading assessments are used to progress monitor over time. There are several types of informal reading and writing assessments teachers can use to progress monitor and make instructional decisions.

▶ Informal Reading Inventory (IRI)

An informal reading inventory (IRI) is an individually administered diagnostic assessment designed to evaluate a number of different aspects of students' reading performance (International Reading Association, n.d.). After reading each leveled passage, a student responds orally to follow-up questions assessing comprehension and recall. These informal reading assessments are used to measure progress and to make instructional decisions based on a student's individual needs.

The types of questions teachers ask during an IRI are:

- Text-based
- Inferential
- Literal
- Main idea
- Key ideas
- Sequence
- Cause and effect
- Plot structure

▶ Running Record

A running record is a way to assess students' oral fluency. These assessments are administered differently depending on what the teacher is trying to measure. However, the basic structure is a student reads from a passage. The teacher has a copy of the same passage. The teacher follows along as the student reads. The teacher marks any errors or miscues the student makes during the reading. The student usually reads for one minute. When the minute is up, the teacher calculates how many correct words per minute the student reads. The teacher and the student can then go over the miscues, decide on next steps, and set new goals.

▶ Informal Writing Tasks

Students can complete informal writing tasks a number of ways: essays, journal entries, story writing, letters, free writing, and others. The main thing to remember when using informal writing assessments is to measure language usage, organization, and mechanics. Then use the qualitative data to make meaningful instructional decisions based on students' individual needs.

QUICK TIP:

On the FTCE Reading K-12 Test, the main reason you would evaluate any type of assessment data is to make instructional decisions in the classroom. Notice that this subskill of Competency 3 states, "Analyze and interpret data from multiple informal and formal reading and writing assessments to guide whole-group instruction." Analyzing data to guide whole-group instruction is data-driven decision making.

4. **Analyze and interpret student data from multiple informal and formal reading and writing assessments to differentiate instruction and develop individual student goals for diverse learners.**

As in all Florida Teacher Certification Exams, the Reading K-12 Test assesses your ability to differentiate instruction based on students' individual needs. Reading teachers use and interpret data from multiple sources to help students reach their learning goals. This data can come from formal and informal assessments.

The assessment used in Florida schools to assess students' English language arts and reading skills is the Florida Standards Assessment (FSA). Achievement levels on the exam range from 1-5. Level 1 is the lowest achievement level, and level 5 is the highest achievement level. Below is a table describing each level. This table was adapted from the Florida Department of Education.

FSA Reading Achievement Levels	
Level 5	This student is above grade level and can easily answer complex questions.
Level 4	This student is likely to excel in the next grade/course.
Level 3	This student may need additional support for the next grade/course.
Level 2	This student is likely to need substantial support for the next grade/course.
Level 1	This student is highly likely to need substantial support for the next grade/course.

- Students who are level 1 and 2 readers need interventions in the form of intensive reading instruction. Interventions should be differentiated and specific based on each student's needs. These students should also be challenged so they continue to make progress.

- Students at a level 3 are considered proficient. However, as indicated in the description of level 3, these students may need additional support to remain proficient. To ensure these students stay proficient and continue to make progress, teachers should monitor these students closely and provide them with challenging reading opportunities.

- Students who are a level 4 or level 5 are above proficiency and are often self-motivated in their learning. Teachers should continually find ways to challenge these students.

Rubrics

A rubric is an evaluation tool or set of guidelines used to promote the consistent application of learning expectations, learning objectives, or learning standards in the classroom, or to measure attainment of information against a consistent set of criteria (The Glossary of Education Reform, 2013). In instructional settings, rubrics clearly define expectations. Rubrics are also used as scoring instruments to determine grades or the degree to which learning standards have been demonstrated or attained by students. Rubrics are often used to assess formal reading and writing assessments. The following is an example of a basic writing rubric.

	1 - Minimal	2 - Meets	3 - Exceeds
Mechanics (Syntactic)	Many spelling, grammar, and punctuation errors; sentence fragments; incorrect use of capitalization.	Some spelling and grammar errors; most sentences have punctuation and are complete; uses uppercase and lowercase letters.	Correct spelling, grammar, and punctuation; complete sentences; correct use of capitalization.
Ideas and Content (Semantic)	Key words are not near the beginning; no clear topic; no beginning, middle, and end; ideas are not ordered.	Main idea or topic is in first sentence; semi-defined topic; attempts beginning, middle and end sections; some order of main idea and details in sequence.	Interesting, well-stated main idea or topic sentence; uses logical plan with an effective beginning, middle, and end; good flow of ideas from topic sentence to details in sequence.
Organization	Ideas are unorganized and do not follow a coherent structure.	Organized enough to read and understand the ideas.	Very organized and easy to understand.

QUICK TIP:

A rubric is the best assessment tool for a performance-based assessment. A rubric sets the criteria and expectations for the task. Students can reference the rubric as they complete the task to make sure they include everything outlined in the rubric. Finally, teachers use the rubric to score and provide feedback to students.

5. Identify characteristics of students at varying reading levels.

In your classroom, you will have students with varying reading levels. It is your job to differentiate instruction based on these varying reading levels. You will have to choose different books and passages that are appropriate for each student and that challenge each student. Text that is at too low of a reading level will bore the student. Text that is at too high of a reading level will frustrate the student. The key is to identify different levels of readiness and reading levels and differentiate accordingly.

Evaluating how many words per minute (wpm) students read is one way to identify their reading level. For example, students should read approximately 60 wpm by the end of first grade, approximately 90 wpm by the end of second grade, and approximately 115 wpm by the end of third grade. The following is a standard chart outlining how many words per minute students should read at what grade level and at what time of the year.

Rasinski (2005) Words Correct Per Minute Target Rates (WPM)			
Grade	Fall	Winter	Spring
1	0-10	10-50	30-90
2	30-80	50-100	70-130
3	50-110	70-120	80-140
4	70-120	80-130	90-140
5	80-130	90-140	100-150
6	90-140	100-150	110-160

QUICK TIP:

Words per minute is only one measure of student reading levels. Teachers must also take into account comprehension. For example, some students may not read quickly, but they may still exhibit comprehension. It is important to use a variety of measures. Those measures include all the assessments discussed in this competency, both formal and informal.

This page intentionally left blank.

1. Which of the following is the most effective way to use a norm-referenced assessment?
   A. To display student progress on the bulletin board.
   B. To make instructional decisions in the classroom.
   C. To measure outcomes of reading programs.
   D. To informally observe students during reading.

2. Which of the following is a criterion-referenced exam?
   A. Pre-assessment
   B. Informal assessment
   C. Standards assessment
   D. Screening

3. A teacher is walking around the room and observing students as they read. This is considered a:
   A. Formative assessment
   B. Summative assessment
   C. Criterion-referenced assessment
   D. Diagnostic assessment

4. A teacher is using a new reading program in her classroom. She wants to measure the program's effectiveness by evaluating outcomes. Which of the following assessments would be most appropriate in this situation?
   A. Criterion-referenced
   B. Norm-referenced
   C. Formative
   D. Summative

5. Assessments used to measure standards mastery and expertise are:
   A. Labs, notebooks, running records, homework assignments
   B. Norm-referenced tests, homework assignments, quizzes
   C. Observations, checklists, surveys
   D. Research papers, presentations, formal debates

6. A teacher is having students engage in a writing project that will take some time over the course of the semester. Which of the following assessment tools will benefit students most so they understand expectations?
   A. Rubric
   B. Formative
   C. Summative
   D. Diagnostic

7. After reading a leveled passage, a teacher asks a student questions; the student responds orally to follow-up questions, and the teacher assesses comprehension and recall. This process is used to measure progress in comprehension and other skills. This type of assessment is called a(n):

    A. Fluency read

    B. Informal reading inventory

    C. Summative assessment

    D. Norm-referenced assessment

8. How does criterion-referenced assessment differ from norm-referenced assessment?

    A. Criterion-referenced assessments measure the average score while the norm-referenced assessments are based on a curve.

    B. Norm-referenced assessments measures student performance against a fixed set of predetermined criteria, and criterion-referenced assessments are designed to compare and rank test takers in relation to one another.

    C. Criterion-referenced measures student performance against a fixed set of predetermined criteria, and norm-referenced assessments are designed to compare and rank test takers in relation to one another.

    D. A criterion-referenced assessment happens throughout learning while a norm-referenced assessment happens at the end of learning.

9. A 4th grade teacher wants to determine her students' knowledge of Civil War before moving to the lesson. Which of the following is the most effective assessment she can use?

    A. Norm-referenced test

    B. Criterion-referenced test

    C. Diagnostic test

    D. Portfolios

10. Which of the following is the most effective way to use formative assessments?

    A. To rank students

    B. To monitor progress

    C. To measure outcomes

    D. To grade on a curve

Competency 3 | Practice Problems Answer Explanations

Number	Answer	Explanation
1.	B	The most effective way to use any assessment is to inform instructional decisions. Remember, data driven decision making will come in many different forms on this test. This question is an example of that.
2.	C	Criterion-referenced exams measure student performance on a set learning criteria or standards. Pre-assessment and informal assessments are considered formative assessments. Screening is used to place students in certain classes or groups.
3.	A	Formative assessments are informal checks to monitor student progress. Observations are considered formative assessments.
4.	D	Summative assessments measure outcomes. Summative assessments come at the end of leaning. To measure if a program worked, ideally, the teacher would administer a pre-assessment, use the program, and then administer a summative assessment. If there was growth from the pre-assessment to the summative, the program is working.
5.	D	When students have mastered the standards, they can apply their knowledge to higher-order thinking activities. Out of all the answer choices, the higher-order thinking activities listed are research papers, presentations, and formal debates. Also, never use homework to assess expertise or mastery; homework is for practice. This eliminates answers A and B. Finally, checklists and surveys in answer choice C do not measure expertise.
6.	A	A rubric is an evaluation tool or set of guidelines used to promote the consistent application of learning expectations, learning objectives, or learning standards in the classroom, or to measure their attainment against a consistent set of criteria. None of the other answer choices convey expectations.
7.	B	An informal reading inventory (IRI) is an individually administered diagnostic assessment designed to evaluate a number of different aspects of students' reading performance. Typically, students read a text and then the teacher asks informal comprehension questions to measure progress.
8.	C	Criterion-referenced exams measure the standards, which is the criteria of the exam. Norm-referenced assessments use a percentile to compare students to other students.
9.	C	A diagnostic test can be used in the beginning of a lesson to determine preconceptions and misconceptions of a topic. Portfolios are collections of work over time. Norm-referenced and criterion-referenced are not appropriate assessments in this situation.
10.	B	Formative assessments are informal assessments used to monitor progress and make instructional decisions.

This page intentionally left blank.

Competency 4 | Knowledge of learning environments and procedures that support reading

1. Apply appropriate grouping practices for specific instructional purposes in reading.

2. Determine appropriate procedures and delivery methods to integrate speaking and listening, reading, writing, and viewing for diverse learners across content areas.

3. Evaluate and select techniques for encouraging motivation and promoting positive attitudes of diverse learners toward academic and personal reading.

4. Apply appropriate instructional methods to integrate technology, support student-centered learning, and establish an information-rich environment.

5. Determine organizational and classroom management practices for multiple reading programs to support diverse learners.

6. Evaluate and select methods of prevention and intervention for students who have not mastered grade-level language arts standards.

1. Apply appropriate grouping practices for specific instructional purposes in reading.

Effective reading teachers use grouping practices to achieve the objective of a lesson. For example, if you want students to evaluate text, you group students in literature circles where the focus is evaluating and discussing the story or passage. If you want students to work on their fluency, you pair students for partner reading. When you want to employ interventions for struggling readers, you group according to skill. Flexible grouping practices are essential in delivering high quality, differentiated, reading instruction.

The main grouping practices used in education are whole-group, small-group, peer pairing/partners, and one-to-one instruction.

Whole Group

This is when teachers are in the front of the room delivering direct instruction. Teachers use whole group method for communicating explicit instructions for an activity or lesson, modeling a skill during reading, and introducing students to a concept or lesson.

Small Group

This is typically referred to as cooperative learning. Small groups are most effective when they have 5 or fewer members. Small-group instruction can consist of students working together in their groups to evaluate text and discuss stories. It can also consist of a teacher-led session where the teacher works with a small group of students to provide specific and targeted reading interventions. Small grouping can be divided into two categories: homogeneous and heterogenous.

▶ **Homogeneous Groups**

Everyone in the group has been identified as having the same reading level. The teacher targets interventions for students in this group who need the same skill. For example, for a group of all level 2 readers who struggle with fluency, the teacher uses fluency strategies during a homogeneous, small-group session.

▶ **Heterogeneous Groups**

Groups are formed so that there is a variety of learning levels and student interests. For example, grouping students by interest rather than reading scores will provide more diversity among the group members.

▶ **One-to-one instruction**

The student works with the teacher individually. This approach is most effective to communicate specific and meaningful feedback on writing assignments. This approach is also effective for fluency interventions.

QUICK TIP:

Students should only be placed in homogeneous groups when a teacher is targeting a specific skill for a selected small group of students for remediation or enrichment. Heterogeneous grouping should be used for all other classroom activities. Keeping students in homogeneous groups limits them. Research supports that **heterogeneous** grouping is most effective.

2. Determine appropriate procedures and delivery methods to integrate speaking and listening, reading, writing, and viewing for diverse learners across content areas.

Integrating speaking, listening, reading, and writing opportunities across content areas is essential in delivering high-quality reading instruction. There numerous delivery methods and resources teachers can use to engage students. The following are a few methods you are most likely to encounter on the FTCE Reading K-12 Test.

Type of Reading	Definition	Example
Basal Reading	Leveled reading books	Dick and Jane series
Guided Reading	Teacher is in charge of the reading process.	The teacher reads a section aloud and then guides another student to read aloud. The teacher is in control of the process.
Shared Reading	The teacher and students share in the process of reading	Partner reading, literature circles
SQ3R	Survey, Question, Read, Recite, Review	Before reading, students look over headings, charts and graphs. Then students turn the headings into questions. Then students read, reread, and review and answer the questions.
Question Answer Relationship (QAR)	QAR is an approach to reading comprehension where students generate reading questions.	While reading, students consider different types of questions, such as think and search questions, main idea questions, and text to self questions.

Type of Reading	Definition	Example
Repeated Reading	Reading text over and over again to help with fluency.	The teacher has a student read a passage and then re-read the passage several times over the course of a week to build automaticity and reading confidence.
Reader's Theater	Reader's theater is a strategy for developing reading fluency. It involves children in oral reading through reading parts in scripts.	Students are reading a story; each student is one of the characters in the book. Students read aloud through the text.
Choral Reading	The students read aloud in unison through a piece of text.	The teacher uses choral reading with ELL students to help them with fluency and confidence.
Silent Sustained Reading (Usually NOT the answer)	Students read silently on their own.	The teacher dedicates 15 minutes every day to having students read their novels on their own.
Popcorn Reading (Usually NOT the answer)	Spontaneously calling on students to read aloud.	The teacher reads. The teacher spontaneously calls out a student's name, and that student reads aloud until the teacher calls on another student.

3. **Evaluate and select techniques for encouraging motivation and promoting positive attitudes of diverse learners toward academic and personal reading.**

The best teachers motivate students by designing and delivering engaging and relevant instruction. Increasing students' motivation to learn is a common theme on the FTCE Professional Education Test. These types of test questions will be presented as scenarios, and you will be expected to choose the most effective approach. Notice the title above—use motivational strategies to engage and challenge *ALL* students. The best teachers motivate all students—high-achieving, low achieving, culturally diverse, and economically diverse students.

While motivation is complex concept, it is helpful to simplify motivation into two distinct types: intrinsic motivation and extrinsic motivation.

INTRINSIC MOTIVATION

Intrinsic motivation is behavior driven by internal rewards rather than external rewards. According to self-determination theory, intrinsic motivation is driven by three things: autonomy, relatedness, and competence.

▶ Autonomy

This has to do with students' independence and self-governance. Allowing students to decide how and what they learn helps to increase autonomy and increase motivation. Students should be permitted to self-select books and work on things that interest them.

▶ Relatedness

Students must see the value in what they are learning as it pertains to their everyday lives. The best teachers make learning relatable and applicable to the real world.

▶ Competence

Students must feel they are equipped to meet your expectations. It is important to challenge students while also providing students with activities based on readiness levels and ability.

EXTRINSIC MOTIVATION

Extrinsic motivation refers to behavior that is driven by external rewards. Providing students with a party if they reach their reading goal or allowing students extra playtime because they cleaned up the classroom are examples of extrinsic motivation. Grades can also be considered extrinsic rewards. Extrinsic motivation is often unsustainable because once the reward is removed, the student is no longer motivated to achieve. The following example shows the way this might be presented on the test.

Example 1 Motivating students

A student scores consistently in the top percentile of the class on tests and quizzes. However, the student rarely interacts with the reading assignments. What can the teacher do to help motivate this student to put effort towards reading time?

A. Allow the student time to go to the library provided he finishes his classwork and homework.

B. Send detailed weekly reports home to his parents so they can encourage him to finish homework.

C. Document how many times he finishes his homework and reward him when he reaches 3 days in a row.

D. Conference with the student and determine activities that will challenge the student while also allowing him to show mastery of the standards.

SOLUTION

Because the student scores well on the tests and quizzes, we can assume the student has mastered the concepts and standards but is unmotivated to compete the classwork and assignments. In this case, we want to be on the lookout for an answer choice where the teacher and the student find a solution by increasing intrinsic motivation for the student. Allowing the student to choose activities increases autonomy, a component of intrinsic motivation. Answer choices A, B and C all highlight extrinsic rewards. While extrinsic rewards work in the short term, they will not be sustainable over time.

Correct Answer: D

CAUTION:

Avoid answer choices that highlight extrinsic rewards. In the real-world, teachers use extrinsic rewards—pizza parties for meeting reading goals, extra time on the computer after students finish their work, candy for getting questions correct, etc. However, on the FTCE Reading K–12 Test, look for the answers that promote intrinsic rather than extrinsic rewards.

4. **Apply appropriate instructional methods to integrate technology, support student-centered learning, and establish an information-rich environment.**

One key phrase in this competency is *student-centered.* The term student-centered learning refers to a wide variety of educational programs, learning experiences, instructional approaches, and academic-support strategies that are intended to address the distinct learning needs, interests, aspirations, or cultural backgrounds of individual students and groups of students. To accomplish this goal, educators use a variety of educational methods, such as modifying assignments and instructional strategies in the classroom and redesigning the ways in which students are grouped and taught in school (The Glossary of Education Reform, 2019).

In a student-centered environment, teachers pay attention to learning preferences, readiness levels, and developmentally appropriate practices. Below are considerations when designing a student-centered or learner-centered classroom environment.

- *Visual learners.* These students thrive when the learning is accompanied by images and graphics to organize information.
- *Auditory learners.* These students grasp concepts best through listening and speaking situations (think lectures and podcasts).
- *Kinesthetic learners.* These students prefer hands-on learning experiences and moving their bodies.
- *Read and write learners*. These students prefer reading and writing activities to make sense of abstract concepts.

Another key phrase in this competency is *information-rich environment.* You should provide students with many opportunities to engage in information in the classroom. Information-rich is also referred to as print-rich, meaning there is an abundance of literary and informational text to use to teach reading among academic disciplines.

Student-centered/information-rich examples

- An English teacher has a classroom library where students can self-select books. The library has informational text and literary text for students to read. The teacher will often ask students to relate what they are currently reading to what they are learning in class. The teacher encourages class discussions about what students are reading and how it relates to their lives.

- A social studies teacher has online and print resources where students can read about current events. The teacher integrates what students are reading in their current events to events in history they are studying in class. The teacher also has students work in discussion groups to read and analyze text and to use text to support students' arguments and claims.

- A health teacher is helping students develop a monthly fitness plan. She guides students through a activity where students use online academic journals to find research about regular exercise and healthy eating. In collaborative groups, students discuss the findings in the research. Then students build an exercise plan based on their interests and what they found in the research.

5. **Determine organizational and classroom management practices for multiple reading programs to support diverse learners.**

The term *diverse learners* means each student has specific needs and teachers must use interventions and supports in reading for students. That means teachers have to have effective classroom management to organize multiple reading programs and interventions.

Teachers with effective classroom management:

- Plan ahead using the state standards.
- Prepare materials before class begins.
- Decide how much time it will take to distribute materials and give instructions.
- Plan a set amount of time to introduce the lesson.
- Decide on the most efficient and effective instructional method for the skills you are teaching.
- Anticipate students' readiness levels.
- Provide adequate time for students to practice the skill(s) taught while being monitored.
- Build in formative assessments and checks along the way.
- Allow time at the end to wrap-up the lesson; closure and debriefing are necessary elements to learning.
- Decide how to move forward by evaluating the data collected during the learning.

On the FTCE Reading K-12 Test, you will be asked questions about effective classroom management that supports multiple reading programs to help multiple students. The following question is how this might look on the exam.

Example 1 Interventions

A teacher has a few students who need specific reading interventions. What would be the most effective way to organize these interventions in the classroom?

A. Have the reading coach work with students who need help and focus instruction to students who have met proficiency.

B. Use a whole group approach to address the reading deficiencies and apply strategies when needed.

C. Set up a variety of reading centers that target reading interventions, use flexible grouping to move students through the centers, and monitor progress by observing students.

D. Group all struggling readers together, apply interventions, and allow grade-level readers to engage in an activity of their choice.

SOLUTION

Answer C has all the good words related to this competency: *target interventions, flexible grouping, monitor progress*. Answer C also accommodates all learners—proficient and struggling. Answer A pushes the responsibility onto the reading coach, which is usually not the correct answer on this test. Answer B is not differentiated at all. In fact, it lumps everyone together, whether they need interventions or not. Finally, answer D uses homogenous grouping in a bad way; the struggling readers are doing work while the on-level readers get to choose their activities. This is not the most effective approach.

Correct Answer: C

---

6. Evaluate and select methods of prevention and intervention for students who have not mastered grade-level language arts standards.

The first thing teachers must consider when planning instruction or planning interventions is the state standards. The standards outline what students must be able to do at each grade level. The second thing teachers must consider when planning instruction or planning interventions is data. Teachers collect this data from informal or formal assessments.

Remember, students who score a level 3 on the state standardized reading test are considered proficient. However, they may still need support. The key phrase in this competency is *mastered grade-level language arts standards.* A student who scores a level 3 has not mastered the standards; the student has met the standard.

FSA Reading Achievement Levels	
Level 5	This student is above grade level and can easily answer complex questions.
Level 4	Likely to excel in the next grade/course
Level 3	May need additional support for the next grade/course
Level 2	Likely to need substantial support for the next grade/course
Level 1	Highly likely to need substantial support for the next grade/course

The following are examples where teachers are effectively implementing prevention and intervention strategies for students who have not yet mastered grade-level standards.

- Before the start of the school year, the teacher reviews the grade-level standards for reading. The teacher also evaluates student data from the state test to determine what skills students are lacking. The teacher looks at specific students and their scores to design and implement targeted interventions for those students. The teacher also comes up with a plan to progress monitor while implementing the interventions.

- A science teacher is using several pieces of data from the semester to determine if a reading strategy is working in the classroom. The assessments the teacher used over the semester were aligned to measure the specific state standards in both science and reading. Based on the data, the teacher will make decisions on how to move forward for the next semester.

This page intentionally left blank.

1. A teacher is putting students with mixed abilities and reading levels. This is called:

   A. Interest grouping

   B. Homogeneous grouping

   C. Heterogeneous grouping

   D. Peer-tutoring grouping

2. A teacher notices a few students are not motivated to read the current section of a piece of informational text. What can the teacher do to motivate students to engage in the reading?

   A. Allow the students to self-select books from a standards-aligned group of informational texts.

   B. Allow students to partner-up and read the text with a buddy.

   C. Reward the students with extra time in the computer lab for finishing the reading.

   D. Require the students to finish the reading for homework.

3. Which of the following is the most effective activity for struggling readers?

   A. Repeated reading

   B. Silent-sustained reading

   C. At-home reading

   D. Popcorn reading

4. Which of the following activities requires students to identify what types of questions go with a reading passage?

   A. Basal reading

   B. QAR

   C. KWL

   D. Reading response journals

5. Which of the following classroom management techniques would help students transition from one center or group activity to another?

   A. Direct instruction

   B. Letters home to parents

   C. Rewards for good behavior

   D. Practiced procedures and protocols

6. A teacher wants to use literature circles in her class. What is the most appropriate structure for organization and instruction?

   A. Whole group to model how to read text aloud

   B. Small group differentiated cooperative learning

   C. Direct instruction to address the entire class

   D. Individual conferencing to set goals

7. A teacher wants to use readers theatre in her class. What is the most appropriate organizational structure for this instructional activity?

   A. Small group text analysis

   B. Direct instruction with modeled reading by the teacher

   C. Whole group with designated roles for reading aloud

   D. Individual conferencing for fluency reading

8. A teacher selects a book for a small group of students to read. Then the teacher provides explicit support to the students. What instructional method is the teacher using?

   A. Basal reading

   B. Shared reading

   C. Popcorn reading

   D. Guided reading

9. After introducing the text to her entire class, the teacher models the reading of the text. Then the students and the teacher read the text together, and following that, they have a discussion about the text. After that, the teacher makes some teaching points, and then a few days later, the reading of the text is repeated. This instructional method is known as:

   A. Guided reading

   B. Basal reading

   C. Choral reading

   D. Shared reading

10. A teacher has several ELL students who are not yet fluent in English. The teacher also has students who are struggling in fluency. Which of the following activities would help these students with fluency, confidence, and reading aloud?

    A. Silent sustained reading

    B. Popcorn reading

    C. Round robin reading

    D. Choral reading

Competency 4 | Practice Problems

Number	Answer	Explanation
1.	C	Heterogeneous groups are formed so that there is a variety of learning levels and student interests. Homogeneous grouping is when students are grouped by the same skill level or reading level. Interest grouping is grouping students based on their interests, which is not indicated in the question. Peer-tutoring grouping is a nonsense answer.
2.	A	Intrinsic motivation is the best answer here. Allowing students to self-select books increases intrinsic motivation. All the other answer choices focus on extrinsic motivators and requirements, which are not as effective as intrinsic motivators.
3.	A	Repeated reading is always a good strategy for struggling readers. Allowing students to reread a piece of text is helpful in developing fluency skills. All the other answer choices are caution words you want to avoid on this exam. Extra homework, silent sustained reading, and repeated vocabulary practice are usually never the correct answers on the FTCE Reading K-12 Test.
4.	B	QAR stands for *question answer relationship* and is the most appropriate answer here. That is what the students are doing in this scenario. KWL charts help activate background knowledge. Basal reading is using level readers. Reading response journals are writing activities where students reflect on their reading.
5.	D	Seamless transitions from one activity to another where students get the maximum amount of learning requires teachers to have good classroom management. This includes practiced procedures and protocols.
6.	B	Literature circles are formal cooperative learning activities where students read and analyze text together. Therefore, B is the best answer. Also, we can eliminate whole group and direct instruction (answers A and C) because they are both similar and address the class in its entirety. Individual conferencing to set goals is not related to the task in the question.
7.	C	Readers theater is when students adapt a text into a script and act out the parts. It is typically done using whole group with everyone having a part in the theater.
8.	D	Guided reading is when the teacher provides explicit support and guides the students in their reading, as described in the question stem. Basal reading uses leveled books to teach basic reading skills. Shared reading is when students share in the process of reading as in partner reads or cooperative learning group reading. Popcorn reading is calling on students spontaneously to read aloud (usually not the correct answer on this test or any FTCE).
9.	D	In this case, the students and the teacher are sharing in the reading process. You might be tempted to choose guided reading. However, guided reading is when the teacher uses explicit instruction and guides students in their reading. Basal reading uses leveled books. Choral reading is when students read together in unison; this helps with fluency.
10.	D	In this case, choral reading is most appropriate because in choral reading, students read aloud in unison. Any mistakes are drowned out by the crowd. Also, choral reading helps with momentum and fluency. Silent sustained reading, popcorn reading, and round robin reading are usually never the answers on this type of exam.

This page intentionally left blank.

Competency 5 | Knowledge of oral and written language acquisition and beginning reading

1. Identify the concepts related to oral and written language acquisition.

2. Identify the concepts related to beginning reading.

3. Apply instructional methods for developing oral language, phonological awareness, concepts of print, alphabet knowledge, and written language development.

1. Identify the concepts related to oral and written language acquisition.

Oral language consists of 6 major areas: phonology, vocabulary, morphology, grammar, pragmatics, and discourse.

1. **Phonology** encompasses the organization of sounds in language.

2. **Vocabulary** (semantics) encompasses both expressive (speaking) and receptive (listening) vocabulary.

3. **Morphology** is the smallest units of meaning in words. An example of morphology is breaking up compound words and analyzing their meaning.

4. **Grammar** (syntax) is the structure of language and words.

5. **Pragmatics** focuses on the social cues or norms in language. This is often referred to as situations in language.

6. **Discourse** focuses on speaking and listening skills in language. Discourse means dialogue.

Cueing Systems

As students begin to read, they use different methods to figure out words. Cueing Systems allow students to use their background knowledge (schema) and apply that to understanding words. There are several types of cues students use when they read.

▶ Semantic Cues

Semantic cues refer to the meaning in language that assists in comprehending texts, including words, speech, signs, symbols, and other meaning-bearing forms. Semantic cues involve the learners' prior knowledge of language. Gradually, students independently relate new information to what is known and personally meaningful.

Example: We were so hungry we had a *picnic* in the park.

Picnic is a strange word, but the student can use the words *hungry* and *park* to figure out the word *picnic*.

▶ Syntactic Cues

Syntactic cues involve the structure of the word as in the rules and patterns of language (grammar), and punctuation. As students read, they use structural cues.

Example: Joey *sat* in class yesterday.

In this case, the student is sure to say *sat* not *sit* because of the word yesterday indicates there needs to be a past tense verb—*sat*.

▶ **Graphophonic Cues**

Graphophonic cues involve the letter-sound or sound-symbol relationships of language. Readers identifying unknown words by relating speech sounds to letters or letter patterns are using graphophonic cues. This process is often called decoding.

Example: The student knows that the word *make* has a long /a/ sound because of the vowel after the *k*. This is a CVCV word.

The following example question is how this might be presented on the FTCE.

Example 1 **Cuing systems**

A teacher is helping students use language structure and grammar to figure out difficult words in grade-level text. The students are using what cueing system?

    A. Semantic

    B. Syntactic

    C. Graphophonic

    D. Phonological

SOLUTION

The students are using language structure and grammar, which is the syntactic cueing system. Semantic is meaning, graphophonic is sound-letter relationships, and phonological is not a suing system.

Correct Answer: B

---

2. Identify the concepts related to beginning reading.

Readers at the beginning (emergent) stage are learning to read and understand words by decoding the reading process as they engage with the text. Emergent literacy involves the skills, knowledge, and attitudes that are developmental precursors to conventional forms of reading and writing (Whitehurst & Lonigan, 1998). Emergent literacy skills begin developing in early infancy and early childhood through participation with adults in meaningful activities involving speaking and reading.

▼ **Pre-Alphabetic Phase**
Students read words by memorizing visual features or guessing words from context.

▼ **Partial-Alphabetic Phase**
Students recognize some letters and can use them to remember words by sight.

▼ **Full-Alphabetic Phase**
Students possess extensive working knowledge of the graphophonemic system, and they can use this knowledge to analyze fully the connections between graphemes and phonemes in words. They can decode unfamiliar words and store fully analyzed sight words in memory.

▼ **Consolidated-Alphabetic Phase**
Students consolidate their knowledge of grapheme-phoneme blends into larger units that recur in different words.

The following example question is how this might look on the exam.

Example 1 Beginning reading

A teacher is using picture cards to help students recognize words. Students see the picture below and say, "Sun!" What phase of word recognition are the students in?

A. Pre-alphabetic
B. Partial- alphabetic
C. Full- alphabetic
D. Consolidated- alphabetic

SOLUTION

The students are only seeing a picture here. Therefore, they are in the pre-alphabetic stage. Partial, full and consolidated all require the use of letter recognition. In this case, there is only a picture.

Correct Answer: A

3. **Apply instructional methods for developing oral language, phonological awareness, concepts of print, alphabet knowledge, and written language development.**

Phonological awareness is an overarching skill that includes identifying and manipulating units of oral language, including parts of words, syllables, onsets, and rimes.

Children who have phonological awareness are able to:

*   identify and make oral rhymes,
*   clap out the number of syllables in a word,
*   recognize words with the same initial sounds like *monkey* and *mother*,
*   recognize the sound of spoken language,
*   blend sounds together (*bl, tr, sk*), and
*   divide and manipulate words.

*Phonological awareness includes 2 very important subskills: phonemic awareness and phonics.

Phonemic awareness is understanding the individual sounds (or phonemes) in words. For example, students who have phonemic awareness can separate the sounds in the word *cat* into three distinct phonemes: /k/, /æ/, and /t/.

Phonics is understanding the relationship between sounds and the spelling patterns (graphemes) representing those sounds. For example, when a student sees that a *c* is followed by an *e, i,* or *y*, the student knows the *c* makes an /s/ sound, as in the words *cycle, circle,* and *receive*.

QUICK TIP:

Think of phonological awareness as the umbrella encompassing many skills students need for literacy: syllabication, onsets, rimes, spelling, etc. Phonemic awareness and phonics are the subskills that support phonological awareness.

Phonemic Awareness	Phonics
Focus on phonemes/sounds	Focus on graphemes/letters and their corresponding sounds
Spoken language	Written language/print
Mostly auditory	Both visual and auditory
Manipulating sounds in words	Reading and writing letters according to sounds, spelling, patterns, and phonological structure

(Heggerty, 2003)

Competency 5 | Practice Problems

1. The teacher is working with emergent readers on word recognition. The students cannot decode words yet. Instead, they are relying on recognizing some letters in the word. The students are in what stage?

   A. Pre-alphabetic

   B. Partial-alphabetic

   C. Full-alphabetic

   D. Consolidated-alphabetic

2. When a student has awareness of phonemes in words, syllables, onset-rime segments, and spelling, he or she is demonstrating:

   A. Phonological awareness

   B. Phonics mastery

   C. Phonemic awareness

   D. Structural analysis

3. Phonemic awareness includes the ability to:

   A. Form compound words and combine word parts

   B. Spell accurately and decode unfamiliar words

   C. Pronounce individual sounds in words

   D. Differentiate between homonyms and spell accurately

4. A student in the partial-alphabetic stage says the word sun by understanding:

   A. All three letters in the word sun: s-u-n

   B. The beginning and ending consonants: S and N

   C. How to decode the word by using grammar rules

   D. How to string together blends in words

5. A teacher is helping students use the semantic cueing system. Which of the following questions aligns with the semantic cueing system?

   A. Is that structured properly?

   B. What sound does that letter make?

   C. Does that make sense?

   D. Is that a long *a* sound or short *a* sound?

6. Which cueing system is the teacher referencing when she discusses the prefixes and suffixes of words?

    A. Semantic

    B. Syntactic

    C. Phonetic

    D. Phonemic

7. Why is teaching phonological generalizations better than teaching phonological rules?

    A. Students don't need to follow all the phonological rules.

    B. Words always follow phonological rules.

    C. Words never follow phonological rules.

    D. Some words don't follow phonological rules.

8. A teacher is teaching words *campfire, popcorn,* and *snowball* to her class. Which of the following is the most effective instructional strategy the teacher can use to teach these vocabulary words?

    A. Semantic analysis

    B. Prefixes and suffixes

    C. Word analysis

    D. Morphological analysis

9. A teacher wants students to understand sounds, spelling, syllables, and structure of a set of words. The teacher is helping students with:

    A. Phonics

    B. Phonemic awareness

    C. Semantics

    D. Phonological awareness

10. Students are breaking up the word below. They are using:

    /p/ /o/ /s/ /i/ /t/ /i/ /v/ /e/

    A. Phonemic awareness

    B. Phonics

    C. Morphology

    D. Semantics

Competency 5 | Practice Problems Answer Explanations

Number	Question	Explanation
1.	B	Because the students can recognize some letters in the word, they are in the partial-alphabetic stage. Pre-alphabetic is no letter recognition. Full-alphabetic is recognizing all letters. Consolidated-alphabetic stage is the most advanced stage.
2.	A	Phonological awareness is putting phonemic awareness and phonics together. Remember, phonological awareness is the umbrella, and phonics and phonemic awareness fall under that umbrella. Structural analysis is not related in this situation.
3.	C	Phonemic awareness involves strictly the sounds in words. In fact, students can practice phonemic awareness without any paper or pencils. It is only the individual sounds (phonemes) in words.
4.	B	Because the student is in the partial-alphabetic stage, the student only knows some of the letters. Answer B is the only answer where the student is using only some of the letters. In this case, it is the consonant sounds in the word.
5.	C	Sematic is using meaning to understand. Therefore, the question, "Does that make sense?" is the most appropriate here. Answers A has to do with a syntactic cueing system. Answers B and D are letter sound relationships, which is graphophonic cueing system.
6.	B	Syntactic cues involve the structure of the word as in the rules and patterns of language (grammar), and punctuation. As students read, they use structural cues. Prefixes and suffixes are part of the structure of the word. Semantic has to do with meaning in the word. Phonetic and phonemic all have to do with the sounds in words.
7.	D	In the English language, some words do not follow all phonological rules. Therefore, teaching phonological generalizations is best because there will always be exceptions to the rules.
8.	D	Morphology is the study of the smallest units of meaning in words. Morphemes are the units of meaning in words. Breaking up compound words by their word parts is morphology.
9.	D	Phonological awareness is all the skills in word analysis: sounds, spelling, syllables, structure, etc. Phonics is just spelling. Phonemic awareness is just sounds. Semantics is meaning.
10.	A	The word is broken up by individual sounds. This is phonemic awareness.

This page intentionally left blank.

Competency 6 | Knowledge of oral and written language acquisition and beginning reading

1. Identify the concepts related to word recognition development.

2. Apply instructional methods for developing phonemic awareness and phonics knowledge for diverse learners.

3. Apply instructional methods for developing word-analysis skills for decoding and encoding monosyllabic and multisyllabic words for diverse learners.

4. Apply instructional methods for promoting the recognition of high frequency words, sight words, and irregularly spelled words for diverse learners.

1. Identify the concepts related to word recognition development.

Phonemes are the smallest units of sounds in words. The word *cat* has three phonemes /c/ /a/ /t/.

Morphology is the study of word structure. Morphemes are the smallest units of meaning in a word. For example, students use prefixes, suffixes and roots to derive meaning. In the word unbelievable, there are three morphemes: **un** (not), **believe**, and **able.**

Syllables are units of pronunciation having one vowel sound, with or without surrounding consonants, forming the whole or a part of a word. For example, there are two syllables in *water (wa-ter)* and three in *elephant (el-e-phant).*

Onsets are the beginning consonant and consonant cluster. For example, the onset for the word **tack** is /t/. The onset for the word **track** is /tr/.

Rimes are the vowel and consonants that follow the onset. For example, in the word **tack** and **track**, the rime is -*ack*.

Common rimes include:

-ack	-ing	-ank	-or
-an	-op	-ay	-ock
-aw	-unk	-ide	-ight
-ick	-ain	-ink	-ame

TEST TIP:

You will most likely encounter questions on the FTCE Reading K-12 Test that have to do with **morphology**. Remember, morphonology is the study of the meaning of words. Morphemes are the smallest units of meaning in a word. Use compound words and prefixes, suffixes, and roots to teach morphology.

2. **Apply instructional methods for developing phonemic awareness and phonics knowledge for diverse learners.**

Students must be able to break down words and understand different components of words. Teachers can help students develop phonemic awareness and phonics by using a number of techniques.

> **QUICK TIP:**
>
> **Phonemic awareness** is the skills that encompass using sounds in words. When you think phonemic awareness, think sounds only. For example, if students are recognizing individual sounds in words or blending sounds in words without having to see the word, it is phonemic awareness.
>
> **Phonics** is understanding the rules of language. Students have to see the letters or words to engage in phonics. For example, in the word **receive**, students know the c makes an /s/ sound. They have to look at the letter c and understand that it is followed by an e, i, or y, and therefore, makes a /s/sound.

▶ **Rhyming**

Rhyming is the repetition of sounds in different words. Students listen to the sounds within words and identify word parts. For example, the /at/ sound in the word mat is the same /at/ sound in cat, rat, sat, and splat.

▶ **Segmentation**

Segmentation is breaking a word apart. This can be done by breaking compound words into two parts, segmenting by onset and rime, segmenting by syllables, or breaking the word into individual phonemes.

Examples of Segmenting		
Compound words	baseball	base ball
Onset and rime	dad	/d/ -/ad/
Syllables	behind	/be-hind/
Individual phonemes	cat	/c/ /a/ /t/
Segmenting phonemes into spoken words	dog	/d/ /o/ /g/

▶ **Isolation**

Isolation means to separate word parts. For example, if the teacher says, "say only the first sound in bat." The students reply with /b/.

▶ **Deletion**

Deletion is omitting a sound in a word or when students take words apart, remove one sound, and pronounce the word without the removed sound (Caldwell, Jennings, & Lerner, 2014). For example, using the word mice, a teacher may ask students to delete the initial /m/ sound, resulting in the word ice. This skill is usually practiced orally.

▶ **Substitution**

Substitution occurs when students replace one sound with another in a word. For example, substitute the first sound in the word *cat* with an /s/ sound. Students say *sat*.

▶ **Blending**

Blending is the ability to string together the sounds that each letter stands for in a word. For example, when students see the word black, they blend the /bl/, the /a/ sound and the ending /k/ sound. Sometimes blending exercises focus just on the consonant blend, like the /br/ sound in the word *brick*.

3. **Apply instructional methods for developing word-analysis skills for decoding and encoding monosyllabic and multisyllabic words for diverse learners.**

Typically, when the FTCE Reading K-12 Test refers to diverse learners, it is referring to students who struggle in reading and students whose first language is not English. Diversity includes socioeconomic statues, interest levels, readiness levels and more. However, on this exam, the term *diverse learners* should signal you to think English language learners (ELL) and struggling readers.

There are a variety of ways to support diverse learners. Most importantly, teachers must differentiate instruction to meet each student's specific needs. Always look for that option on the exam. After that, there are specific areas to support students. Try to think of the sequence of language acquisition when deciding how to help students.

Stages of second language acquisition

1. **Pre-production.** The learner watches and listens in an attempt to absorb the language. It is also referred to as "the silent stage."

2. **Early production.** The learner starts to use some words but has not yet mastered forming sentences. Using pictures (just as in first language acquisition) is helpful in this stage.

3. **Speech emergence.** The learner uses simple sentences that may or may not be correct. He or she begins to understand simple phrases in this stage.

4. **Intermediate fluency.** The learner has a much better grasp on the language as he/she begins to comprehend information taught in the second language and speaks in longer sentences.

5. **Advanced fluency.** The learner can speak and understand the new language with little to no support. This is when students demonstrate cognitive language proficiency to go beyond the basics and think/ respond critically in the acquired language.

Beyond the stages of second language acquisition, most students go through the following sequence when learning to read. Oral fluency (phonemic awareness) is typically the first step. Then the student can start to engage with phonics and phonological awareness.

Decoding words comes after phonemic awareness because decoding words requires phonics skills. The following tables outline different ways in which teachers use phonics to help students decode monosyllabic and multisyllabic words.

Grapheme Type	Definition	Examples
Single letters	A single consonant letter can be represented by a phoneme.	B, d, f, g, h, j, k, l, m, n, p, r, s, t, v, w, y, z
Doublets	A doublet uses two of the same letter to spell a consonant phoneme.	ff, ll, ss, zz
Digraphs	Digraphs are a two-letter (di-) combinations that create one phoneme.	Th, sh, ch, wh, ph, ng (sing) gh (cough) ck
Trigraphs	Trigraphs are three-letter (tri-) combinations that create one phoneme.	-tch -dge
Diphthong	Diphthongs are sounds formed by the combination of two vowels in a single syllable, in which the sound begins as one vowel and moves toward another. They can appear in the initial, middle or final position in a word.	aisle coin loud buy
Consonant blends	Consonant blends include two or three graphemes, and the consonant sounds are separate and identifiable.	s-c-r (scrape) c-l (clean) l-k (milk)
Silent letter combinations	Silent letter combinations use two letters: one represents the phoneme and the other is silent.	kn (knock) wr (wrestle) gn (gnarl)
Combination *qu*	These two letters always go together and make a /kw/ sound.	quickly
Single letters	A single vowel letter that stands for a vowel sound.	(short vowels) cat, hit, gem, pot, sub (long vowels) me, no, mute
Vowel teams	Vowel teams are combinations of two, three, or four letters that stand for a vowel sound.	(short vowels) head, hook (long vowels) boat, sigh, weigh (diphthongs) soil, bout

The following table is helpful when identifying consonant and vowel rules of phonics.

Syllable Type	Description	Example
Closed	A syllable with a single vowel followed by one or more consonants. The vowel is closed in by a consonant. The vowel sound is usually short.	Cat bat clock letter
Open	A syllable that ends with a single vowel. The vowel is not closed in by a consonant. The vowel is usually long. The letter *y* acts like a vowel.	go no fly he
Vowel- Consonant-Silent e	A syllable with a single vowel followed by a consonant then the vowel *e*. The first vowel sound is long, and the final *e* is silent. Can be referred to as the sneaky silent *e*.	bike skate kite poke
Vowel Teams	A syllable that has two consecutive vowels. Vowel teams can be divided into two types: • Long vowel teams: Two vowels that make one long vowel sound. • Variant vowel teams: Two vowels that make neither a long nor a short vowel sounds but rather a variant. Letters *w* and *y* act as vowels.	Long vowel teams: eat, seat, say, see Variant vowel teams: stew, paw, book Exceptions: bread (makes a short vowel sound)
R-controlled	A syllable with one or two vowels followed by the letter *r*. The vowel is not long or short. The *r* influences or controls the vowel sound.	car far her fur sir
Consonant le (-al, -el) Final stable	A syllable that has a consonant followed by the letters *le*, *al*, or *el*. This is often one syllable. This is the only syllable type without the vowel sound.	ta<u>ble</u> sta<u>ble</u> lo<u>cal</u>
Other Final Stable Syllables	A syllable that makes one sound at the end of a word. Examples include: *sion, tion, ture, sure, age, cious, tious*.	ten<u>sion</u>, na<u>tion</u>, cul<u>ture</u>, compo<u>sure</u>, ram<u>page</u>, gra<u>cious</u>, infec<u>tions</u>

The following table includes syllable patterns.

Syllable Pattern	Description	Example
CVC	consonant-vowel-consonant	bat, cat, tap
CVCV	consonant-vowel-consonant-vowel	make, take, bake
CCVC	consonant-consonant-vowel-consonant	trap, chop, grit
CVCC	consonant-vowel-consonant-consonant	tack, hunt, fast

Example **1** **Literacy stages**

Example 1 — Literacy stages

Which of the following would be the most appropriate first step to engage diverse learners at the emergent stage of literacy?

    A. Have student analyze and discuss text in literature circles.

    B. Have students memorize sight words.

    C. Develop students' oral fluency.

    D. Use phonics to help students decode words.

SOLUTION

Remember, oral fluency is usually the *first* skill students develop. Because the question asks about the *first step*, answer C is most appropriate here. Answer A is a high-level skill, and students will need to be fluent in order to achieve that objective. Answer B is simply memorization and usually not a great answer for the exam. Answer D is part of emergent literacy. However, it is above oral fluency.

Correct Answer: C

---

4. **Apply instructional methods for promoting the recognition of high frequency words, sight words, and irregularly spelled words for diverse learners.**

High-frequency words are also referred to as sight words. These words occur most often in grade-level texts. Some sight words do not follow English language rules and cannot be sounded out. To read on grade level, students must have automaticity with high frequency words. These words should be memorized because they occur frequently. Examples include:

• want	• said	• by	• why
• what	• see	• are	• there

Decodable words can be sounded out and follow letter-sound correspondence and spelling conventions or rules. For example, a student can decode the word *expect* by segmenting the word: *ex-pe-ct*. It is not a word that occurs often like the word *said* or *there*. Therefore, a student may have to take a few seconds to decode the word.

1. A teacher is using the following instructional practices.

   - Teach students to break words down by individual sounds.
   - Teach students to focus on sounds as they rhyme words.

   What is the focus of the teacher's instruction?

   A. Phonemic awareness

   B. Decoding

   C. Phonics

   D. Structural analysis

2. Which of the following would be the most appropriate activity for a student who struggles with several high-frequency words?

   A. Have the student write the words over and over again.

   B. Provide the student with a bank of the high frequency words for memorization.

   C. Have the student discuss the words with a partner.

   D. Post the sight words on a word wall.

3. Which word is correctly broken up by onset and rime?

   A. /mon/ -/key/

   B. /t/- /ap/

   C. /hand/- /y/

   D. /pro/-/tect/

4. A teacher is working with a student on initial sounds. The teacher says pet and asks the student to replace the initial consonant to make other words, such as get, vet, and set. What is this an example of?

   A. Segmenting

   B. Blending

   C. Structural analysis

   D. Substituting

5. Which of the following set of words is most appropriate if the teacher is focusing on morphology during reading instruction?

   A. Pizza, system, tragedy

   B. Track, trade, trophy

   C. Cat, bat, sat

   D. Unbelievable, irreplaceable, disrespectful

6. Which of the following is a CVCV word?

    A. Crank

    B. Mat

    C. Mate

    D. Believe

7. A teacher is explaining that some words occur frequently in text, and some do not follow the rules of phonics. Which instructional approach would be most effective here?

    A. Use word analysis.

    B. Use phonemic awareness.

    C. Use sight word memorization.

    D. Use decoding strategies.

8. Students have issues with segmentation. What is the most appropriate instructional approach?

    A. Have students break apart words by separate phonemes.

    B. Have students break apart compound words

    C. Have students blend beginning consonants together.

    D. Have students use prefixes and suffixes to learn words.

9. A teacher wants to help students develop rhyme. What is the most appropriate instructional approach?

    A. Teach students to focus on words that end in *ing*.

    B. Teach students words that have the same prefix.

    C. Teach students to blend the beginning of words.

    D. Teach students to use CVC words.

10. Students are struggling with syllabication. What is the most appropriate instructional approach?

    A. Divide compound words by meaning.

    B. Show students how words can sound the same.

    C. Divide words and clap the different parts of the word.

    D. Have students substitute different sounds in words.

Competency 6 | Practice Problems Answer Explanations

Number	Answer	Explanation
1.	A	Working with individual sounds in words is phonemic awareness. Answers B, C and D all focus on phonics, which means students have to see the words and apply spelling rules. That is not what's happening in the activities listed.
2.	B	The term *high frequency words* is another word for sight words. Students have to memorize these words because the words do not follow typical phonics and they occur frequently the text.
3.	B	Onset is the beginning consonant and consonant cluster. Rime is the vowel and consonants that follow. In this case, the only answer choice with a definitive onset and rime is B. The /t/ is the onset. The /ap/ is the rime. The other answer choices are broken up by syllables, not onset and rime.
4.	D	The key word in the question is *replace*. *Replace* also means *substitute*. The students are changing out, replacing, or substituting one sound for another in this activity.
5.	D	Morphology is the study of the structure of words. Using prefixes, roots and suffixes is a way to use morphology. The only answer choice that uses prefixes, roots and suffixes is answer D.
6.	C	C stands for consonant. V stands for vowel. The word mate is a CVCV word. Crank is a CCVCC word. Mat is a CVC word. The word believe does not fit here.
7.	C	High frequency words are sight words and should be memorized. Sight words occur frequently in the text and some do not follow the rules of phonics. It is most effective for students to memorize these words rather than trying to decode them or sound them out.
8.	A	Segmenting is breaking apart a word by individual sounds (phonemes). This helps students with phonemic awareness. Answer B and D are exercises in morphology. Segmenting is the opposite of blending, which eliminates answer C.
9.	A	Helping students rhyme the ending syllables is helpful, and using *ing* at the end of the words is an easy way to model rhyming. Answers B, C, and D do not have to do with rhyming.
10.	C	One of the most common ways to teach syllabication is to chunk the words into syllables and clap the different parts of the word. For example, in the word believe, student clap and say /be/ and then clap and say /lieve/.

This page intentionally left blank.

Competency 7 | Knowledge of oral and written language acquisition and beginning reading

1. Identify the concepts of vocabulary acquisition and use.

2. Evaluate and select instructional methods for vocabulary acquisition and use in speaking and listening, reading, and writing for diverse learners.

3. Apply appropriate instructional methods for developing the use of independent word learning strategies for diverse learners.

4. Apply appropriate instructional methods for developing and using conversational, general academic, and domain-specific words and phrases for diverse learners.

1. Identify the concepts of vocabulary acquisition and use.

When students begin to read, they acquire vocabulary skills. These skills progress in order: listening, speaking, reading, writing.

Listening vocabulary. First students acquire listening vocabulary. Listening vocabulary refers to the words we need to know to understand what we hear. This is part of students' receptive vocabulary.

Speaking vocabulary. Next, students acquire speaking vocabulary. Speaking vocabulary consists of the words we use when we speak. This is part of students' expressive vocabulary.

Reading vocabulary. Next, students acquire reading vocabulary. Reading vocabulary refers to the words we need to know to understand what we read. This is part of students' receptive vocabulary.

Writing vocabulary. The last skill acquired is writing vocabulary. Writing vocabulary consists of the words we use in writing. This is part of students' expressive vocabulary.

Receptive Vocabulary vs Expressive Vocabulary		
Receptive	Reading, Listening	Listening to a book on tape, reading an article
Expressive	Speaking, Writing	Engaging in role play, writing poem

2. **Evaluate and select instructional methods for vocabulary acquisition and use in speaking and listening, reading, and writing for diverse learners.**

There are a variety of ways to approach vocabulary instruction. Teaching vocabulary in context is essential. However, students must also use definitions and parts of speech to figure out words. Just like all instruction, vocabulary instruction should be differentiated to meet the specific needs of every student and. The following are the findings of the National Reading Panel's research. You will find scenarios with these types of approaches in the correct answers on the FTCE Reading K-12 Test.

- Intentional instruction of vocabulary items is required for specific texts.

- Repetition and multiple exposures to vocabulary items are important.

- Learning in rich contexts is valuable for vocabulary learning. Vocabulary tasks should be restructured as necessary.

- Vocabulary learning should entail active engagement in learning tasks.

- Computer technology can be used effectively to help teach vocabulary.

- Vocabulary can be acquired through incidental learning. How vocabulary is assessed and evaluated can have differential effects on instruction.

- Dependence on a single vocabulary instructional method will not result in optimal learning.

3. **Apply appropriate instructional methods for developing the use of independent word learning strategies for diverse learners.**

An important thing to keep in mind when thinking about vocabulary instruction is to use activities that use new vocabulary in an authentic, real-world manner. While dictionaries are useful tools and glossaries provide support, they should not be the only mode of teaching vocabulary. The following are does and don'ts regarding vocabulary instruction.

Do	Don't
Have students use context to figure out difficult words.	Have students write words over and over again.
Use interactive word walls so students can engage with new vocabulary.	Have students copy definitions from the glossary.
Model think aloud strategies for students to use when faced with difficult academic and domain specific words.	Assign extra vocabulary homework for those who struggle.

QUICK TIP:

Learning vocabulary in context is also referred to as **incidental vocabulary**. Incidental vocabulary learning is the unintended learning of words that occurs in the course of engagement in other activities. This is the real-world application of vocabulary and is regarded by some scholars as the most effective form of word learning.

Stages of vocabulary acquisition for ELL students

It is important to remember ELL stages of language acquisition for this section of the FTCE Reading K-12 Test.

Stage	Description
Stage 1: Pre-Production	This is commonly known as the silent period. At this stage, students are listening and deciphering vocabulary. Students may have receptive vocabulary (listening), but they are not speaking yet. In this stage, students benefit from repetition when trying to understand new words and phrases.
Stage 2: Early Production	This stage can last up to six months. Students at this stage understand about 1000 words in the new language. Students begin to form short phrases that may be grammatically incorrect. Students at this stage will use pictures to represent ideas in the new language.
Stage 3: Speech Emergence	At this stage, students will start to communicate with simple phrases and sentences. Students understand up to 3000 words during this stage. Students also begin to develop comprehension in the new language (L2).
Stage 4: Intermediate Fluency	During this stage, students have a robust vocabulary in the second language—6000 or more words. Students begin to communicate effectively in their writing and speech.
Stage 5: Advanced Fluency	At this stage, students are proficient and have comprehension and critical thinking in the second language. It can take 4–10 years for students to achieve academic proficiency in a second language.

4. **Apply appropriate instructional methods for developing and using conversational, general academic, and domain-specific words and phrases for diverse learners.**

Vocabulary differs from content area to content area. Words in science class are much different than the words used in English class. Those words are different that words used in general conversation. Teachers must prepare students to engage with conversation, general academic, and domain specific words.

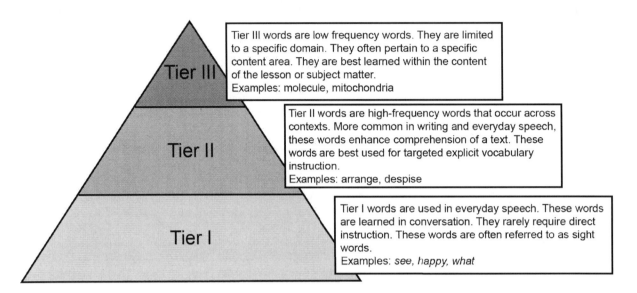

Tier III words are low frequency words. They are limited to a specific domain. They often pertain to a specific content area. They are best learned within the content of the lesson or subject matter.
Examples: molecule, mitochondria

Tier II words are high-frequency words that occur across contexts. More common in writing and everyday speech, these words enhance comprehension of a text. These words are best used for targeted explicit vocabulary instruction.
Examples: arrange, despise

Tier I words are used in everyday speech. These words are learned in conversation. They rarely require direct instruction. These words are often referred to as sight words.
Examples: *see, happy, what*

TEST TIP:

On the FTCE Reading K-12 Test, you are likely to come across questions about vocabulary while promoting content area literacy. Remember, science, social science, and math texts all contain complex vocabulary. Be sure to choose answers that promote teaching vocabulary **in context**, meaning relating it to the overall task at hand. Copying words from a dictionary or glossary is typically not the best approach. Using context in vocabulary instruction is another way of promoting relevance.

Competency 7 | Practice Problems

1. Which type of vocabulary do students acquire first?

    A. listening

    B. speaking

    C. reading

    D. writing

2. Which is NOT a best practice for vocabulary instruction?

    A. Model using context clues

    B. Teaching prefixes, suffixes, and roots

    C. Explicit instruction using a dictionary

    D. Using word walls for target vocabulary

3. Which of the following words would be considered a tier 1 word?

    A. See

    B. Vulnerable

    C. Mitochondria

    D. Suspect

4. Which of the following methods would be most appropriate for a teacher to measure students' mastery of vocabulary words?

    A. Use a multiple-choice test.

    B. Have students participate in a vocabulary game.

    C. Have students memorize definitions.

    D. Have students apply the vocab in a writing assignment.

5. What would be the most effective way to engage learners in conversational and general academic words?

    A. Writing assignment

    B. Role-play

    C. Reading aloud

    D. Sight word memorization

6. Students are talking loudly as they enter the classroom. The teacher says, "Don't bring that cacophony into my class!" What type of vocabulary application is the teacher using?

    A. The teacher is using incidental vocabulary instruction.

    B. The teacher is using systematic vocabulary instruction.

    C. The teacher is using accidental vocabulary instruction.

    D. The teacher is using direct vocabulary instruction.

7. Publishing companies use italics or bold to indicate important words. How are these presented in the book?

    A. In the appendix

    B. In the glossary

    C. At the end of the chapter

    D. At the beginning of the chapter

8. Which of the following would be most effective in teaching students tier III words in a biology class?

    A. Have students copy words from the glossary.

    B. Have students use vocabulary words in a five-paragraph essay.

    C. Have students use an interactive word wall to use words in context.

    D. Have students circle the vocabulary words in a piece of text.

9. A teacher wants to work on students' expressive vocabulary. What would be the most effective activity?

    A. Reading and writing

    B. Speaking and listening

    C. Listening and reading

    D. Speaking and writing

10. Which of the following group of words would be best memorized?

    A. believe, receive, piece

    B. artillery, battle, weaponry

    C. irregular, immoral, inadequate

    D. would, said, read

Competency 7 | Practice Problems Answer Explanations

Number	Answer	Explanation
1.	A	Listening vocabulary Speaking vocabulary Reading vocabulary Writing vocabulary
2.	C	Vocabulary should never be taught using a dictionary. A dictionary can be used as a support or tool but should never be the center of the activity. Answers A, B and D are all effective in teaching vocabulary. Remember, effective vocabulary instruction allows students to apply the words in context (answer A), uses structure to figure out meaning (answer B), and helps students to interact with words authentically (answer D).
3.	A	Tier I words are used in everyday speech. These words are learned in conversation. They rarely require direct instruction. These words are often referred to as sight words. Tier II words are seen in across contexts as in answer B (vulnerable) and D (suspect). Tier III words are domain specific and occur in certain content areas, as in answer C (mitochondria).
4.	D	Application is the way to show mastery. Applying skills to a task is a high-level activity. Therefore, D is the best answer. Multiple choice tests, games and memorization are not effective in measuring mastery.
5.	B	The key word in the question stem is conversational. Role play is the best activity for that. Also, general academic language is the kind of language students would use in conversation. Reading aloud, sight word memorization and writing assignments will not help students use conversational vocab.
6.	A	Incidental vocabulary learning is the unintended learning of words that occurs in the course of engagement in other activities. This is the real-world application of vocabulary and is regarded by some scholars as the most effective form of word learning.
7.	B	Typically, words that are bolded or italicized in the text are presented as vocabulary words in the glossary.
8.	C	Answer C has all the good words when it comes to vocabulary: *interactive, word wall, in context.*
9.	D	Expressive vocabulary is used to express words. Speaking and writing are expressive activities. Listening and reading are receptive activities.
10.	D	Answer D has a group of words that are considered sight words, and these words should be memorized. Answer A has a group of words that follow the rules for *c*. Answer B is a group of tier III words, and these words should not be memorized. Answer C uses prefixes and are not sight words.

This page intentionally left blank.

Competency 8 | Knowledge of reading fluency and reading comprehension

1. Identify the components of reading fluency that support comprehension.

2. Apply appropriate instructional methods for developing fluent reading with purpose and understanding for diverse learners.

3. Evaluate and select instructional methods for teaching skills and developing strategies for comprehension and analysis of informational texts.

4. Evaluate and select instructional methods for teaching skills and developing strategies for comprehension and analysis of literary texts.

5. Apply instructional methods for developing metacognition and critical thinking for diverse learners.

6. Apply instructional methods for engaging students in evidence-based collaborative discussions about literary and informational print and nonprint texts.

7. Apply instructional methods to develop study skills for comprehension of literary and informational texts for diverse learners.

1. Identify the components of reading fluency that support comprehension.

Fluency is defined as the ability to read with speed, accuracy, and proper expression, and it is a necessary skill for reading comprehension. For students to understand text, they must first read through the text with fluency. This way they can focus on meaning rather than sounding out words.

Comprehension is the essence of reading. This is when students begin to form images in their minds as they read. They are able to predict what might happen next in a story because they understand what is happening in the story. Students who are in the comprehension stage of reading do not need to decode (sound out) words. They read **fluently** with **prosody**, **automaticity**, and **accuracy**.

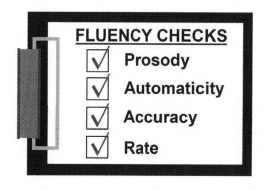

Teachers perform **fluency checks** or **fluency reads** to measure students' reading progress. While the student reads, the teacher follows along. As the student reads, the teacher checks for **automaticity**, which is effortless, speedy word recognition. The teacher also checks the student's **accuracy** and **rate**.

- **Prosody** – comprises timing, phrasing, emphasis, and intonation that readers use to help convey aspects of meaning and to make their speech lively. Prosody includes stopping at periods, pausing at commas, reading with inflection, and reading with expression.

- **Automaticity** - is the fast, effortless word recognition that comes with repeated reading practice. When students are reading at > 95% accuracy, they have automaticity.

- **Accuracy** – is the amount of words a student reads correctly. Typically, accuracy is measured by having students read aloud during a fluency read (also called a running record). The student reads and the teacher marks any words the student miscues.

- **Rate** – is the speed at which students read words correctly. Rate is typically expressed in correct words per min (wpm).

Fluency and Cognitive Endurance

Fluency supports cognitive endurance. When students have the cognitive endurance to read through large sections of text and build meaning from that text, students are not wasting cognitive energy on decoding words. Instead, students are reading fluently, using their cognitive energy towards comprehension and critical thinking.

According to Lyon and Moats (1997), a young reader has only so much attentional capacity and cognitive energy to devote to a particular task. If the reading of the words on the page is slow and labored, readers simply cannot remember what they have read, much less relate the ideas they have read about to their own background knowledge. Fluent readers use less cognitive energy and are able to spend more time developing comprehension on the reading, rather than decoding words. Meaning and understanding of words can be lost in the decoding phase. That is why building automaticity and cognitive endurance is essential in developing comprehension.

2. **Apply appropriate instructional methods for developing fluent reading with purpose and understanding for diverse learners.**

As previously mentioned, fluency is important because it allows students to use cognitive energy on building comprehension of text, rather than using cognitive energy on sounding out words. All of the following strategies are effective for English language learners (ELLs) as well.

▶ Choral Reading

Reading aloud in unison with a whole class or group of students. Choral reading helps build students' fluency, self-confidence, and motivation. Choral reading can be done in a variety of ways.

- **Unison** – The whole class reads together in unison.
- **Refrain** – One student reads the narrative part of the text; the rest of the class reads the refrain.
- **Antiphon** – The class is divided in two groups; one group reads one part, and the other group reads the other part.

▶ Repeated Reading

Reading passages again and again, aiming to read more words correctly per minute each time, helps to increase automaticity.

▶ Running Records

Following along as a student reads and marking when he or she makes a mistake or miscues. At the end, the teacher counts how many words per min (wpm) the student read correctly.

▶ Miscue Analysis

Looking over the running record, analyzing why the student miscued, and employing strategies to help the student with miscues.

▶ Conferencing

Conferencing individually with students to go over fluency goals and strategies is very effective. Teachers and students can look over fluency data and decide how to move forward to build better fluency.

▶ Data folders

Often, students will keep their fluency data in a data folder. It is effective to chart progress over time so students can see their growth. Data should be kept confidential and only discussed between the teacher, student and parents.

The following question is how developing fluency might be presented on the exam.

Example 1 Developing fluency

A teacher encourages 2nd grade ELL students to take a decodable passage home and read it 2 times each night for 5 nights. The primary purpose of this strategy would be to increase:

    A. Comprehension

    B. Phonics

    C. Automaticity

    D. Metacognition

SOLUTION

This is a repeated reading exercise. Repeated reading helps to increase automaticity and fluency.

Correct Answer: C

3. **Evaluate and select instructional methods for teaching skills and developing strategies for comprehension and analysis of informational texts.**

Informational text is nonfiction text written with the intention to inform the reader. Social studies, science, math and other content areas provide an opportunity to use informational text.

Question Answer Relationships (QAR). Students categorize the types of reading questions. This occurs usually during reading comprehension assessments where students read a piece of text and then answer leveled questions. The QAR categorizes questions in 4 ways:

1. *Right there*. These are literal questions with answers that can be found directly in the text. Teachers will often say, "You can point to these answers directly in the text."

2. *Think and search*. Answers are gathered from several parts of the text and put together to make meaning.

3. *Author and you*. For these questions, students are required to relate it to their own experience to the reading. This can also be referred to as text-to-self. They have to use their schema or background knowledge to answer these questions.

4. *On my own*. These questions do not require the student to have read the passage, but he/she must use their background or prior knowledge to answer the question.

▶ **SQ3R**

This is a comprehensive reading activity that stands for:

- **Survey** – scan titles, headings, charts, graphs, etc. to get a feel for the entire text.
- **Question** – As the students survey, they turn the headings into questions.
- **Read** – Students read the text for comprehension.
- **Recite** – Students begin to answer the questions they generated.
- **Review** – Students summarize what they have read.

▶ **Cooperative learning**

Using small groups to allow students to read and analyze text together. Cooperative learning is most effective when it is structured and when every student has a role in the outcome of the reading activity.

▶ **Domain specific vocabulary**

Focusing on complex vocabulary specific for the informational text and using those words in context.

▶ **Background knowledge**

It is important to activate students' background knowledge before reading complex informational text. This can be done a variety of ways. However, on the FTCE Reading K-12 Test, the most common activity to activate background knowledge is a KWL chart. The following is an example of a KWL chart. The **K** in the chart stands for what students already **KNOW** already about the topic. The **K** is the background knowledge.

K	W	L
What do I already know?	What do I want to learn?	What did I learn?
Cells are small.	What do cells do?	Parts of the cell and how they interact to support life

4. **Evaluate and select instructional methods for teaching skills and developing strategies for comprehension and analysis of literary texts.**

Literary text is fiction that is narrative or tells a story. There are an infinite number of instructional approaches for teaching comprehension of literary texts. The following are a few that are present on most the FTCE Reading K-12 Test.

Activity	Definition	Example
Jigsaw	A cooperative learning activity in which each student or groups of students read and analyze a small piece of information that is part of a much larger piece. They then share what they learned with the class.	Teachers arrange students in groups. Each group reads and analyzes a piece of a text. Group members then join with members of other groups, and each student shares and discusses his or her section of the text. As the group shares, the entire text is covered. It is referred to as Jigsaw because students complete the puzzle when they share their individual pieces.
Chunking	A reading activity that involves breaking down a difficult text into manageable pieces.	In a science class, students break down a lengthy and complex chapter on genetics by focusing on pieces of the text. The teacher has planned for students to read and analyze the text one paragraph at a time.
Think-Pair-Share	A cooperative learning activity in which students work together to solve a problem or answer a question.	**Think** – The teacher asks a specific question about the text. Students "think" about what they know or have learned about the topic. **Pair** – Students pair up to read and discuss. **Share** – Students share what they've learned in their pairs. Teachers can then expand the "share" into a whole-class discussion.

Activity	Definition	Example
Reading Response Journals	A writing activity where students use journals to react to what they read by expressing how they feel and asking questions about the text.	After reading a chapter of a book in class, the teacher asks students to use their reading response journals to respond to the story emotionally, make associations between ideas in the text and their own ideas, and record questions they may have about the story.
Evidence-Based Discussion	The teacher sets the expectation that students use evidence in the text to support claims they make during the discussion.	The class is discussing World War II. Students are asking and answering questions. When making claims, students identify support for those claims in the text.
Literature Circles	A small-group, cooperative learning activity where students engage and discuss a piece of literature/text.	In their cooperative groups, students read and analyze text together. Each student contributes to the learning. There is an administrator who decides when to read and when to stop and discuss. There is a note taker who writes down important information. There are 2 readers who take turns reading the text based on the administrator's suggestions.

5. **Apply instructional methods for developing metacognition and critical thinking for diverse learners.**

One of the most important things you can do as a certified teacher is align your instruction to the state adopted standards. Once you have aligned your instruction to the standards, the next step is to find ways to foster critical, creative, and reflective thinking.

The other important aspect of your instruction is your ability to elicit critical, higher order thinking in your students.

TEST TIP:

Standards always come first, especially on the FTCE Reading K-12 Test. The state wants to ensure that everything you do in the classroom is aligned to the standards. Therefore, if you see an answer choice that says anything about the state standards, it is most likely the correct answer.

▶ Critical Thinking

This is multi-step, high-level thinking. Students are stretching in their thinking to analyze, evaluate, interpret, and synthesize information to reach a conclusion or make a judgment.

▶ Creative Thinking

This requires students to create something by applying their skills. When students apply their skills, they are operating at a high cognitive level.

▶ Reflective Thinking

Students look back on and reflect upon their learning process to promote abstract thinking and to encourage the application of learning strategies to new situations.

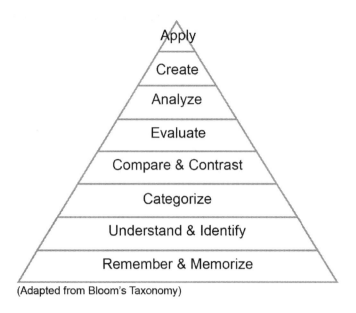

(Adapted from Bloom's Taxonomy)

Bloom's Taxonomy

Bloom's Taxonomy is a hierarchical model used to classify educational learning objectives into levels of complexity and specificity. The higher up the pyramid, the more complex the thinking skills. The skills are represented as verbs on the pyramid. When answering questions on the FTCE Reading K-12 Test regarding critical thinking, reference Bloom's Taxonomy. The figure above is a modified version of Bloom's Taxonomy. We have modified it to include other skills (verbs) you may see on the exam.

The skills (verbs) at the highest points of the pyramid are evaluate, analyze, create, and apply. When you are faced with a critical thinking problem on the test, visualize this pyramid, and look for answer choices that reflect the higher portions of the pyramid.

Metacognition is thinking about thinking. When students have metacognition, they understand the processes in their minds and can employ a variety of techniques to understand text.

Strategies for boosting **comprehension**, **critical thinking**, and **metacognition** are:

- *Predicting.* Asking students what they think will happen next.
- *Questioning.* Having students ask questions based on what they are reading.
- *Read aloud/think aloud.* Teacher or student reads and stops to think aloud about what the text means.
- *Summarizing.* Asking students to summarize what they just read in their own words.

6. Apply instructional methods for engaging students in evidence-based collaborative discussions about literary and informational print and nonprint texts.

A major shift in English language arts standards is the emphasis on reading, writing, and speaking grounded in evidence from texts, both literary and informational. The following is taken from the Common Core State Standards (CCSS) Key shifts in English Language Arts page on the CCSS website. We feel this is important because it is a comprehensive explanation of what evidence-based discussion and writing look like in the classroom.

Reading, writing, and speaking <u>grounded in evidence</u> from texts, both literary and informational

The Common Core emphasizes using evidence from texts to present careful analyses, well-defended claims, and clear information. Rather than asking students questions they can answer solely from their prior knowledge and experience, the standards call for students to answer questions that depend on their having read the texts with care.

The reading standards focus on students' ability to read carefully and grasp information, arguments, ideas, and details based on evidence in the text. Students should be able to answer a range of text-dependent questions, whose answers require inferences based on careful attention to the text.

Frequently, forms of writing in K–12 have drawn heavily from student experience and opinion, which alone will not prepare students for the demands of college, career, and life. Though the standards still expect narrative writing throughout the grades, they also expect a command of sequence and detail that are essential for effective argumentative and informative writing. The standards' focus on evidence-based writing along with the ability to inform and persuade is a significant shift from current practice.

TEST TIP:

If you see anything related to evidence-based writing or discussion in one of the answer choices on the exam, it is the correct answer. Teachers must help **students support claims made in both** writing and speaking with evidence from the text.

7. **Apply instructional methods to develop study skills for comprehension of literary and informational texts for diverse learners.**

Teachers must use a balanced literacy approach in the classroom. This means they are using both informational and literary texts. On the FTCE Reading K-12 Test, be on the lookout for answers that outline teachers using both literary and informational text in the content area to support reading across disciplines. The following is how this might look on the exam.

Example **1** **Instructional methods**

An 8th grade health teacher wants students to read a news article about a new health study involving teens and sleep. The teacher knows the text will be complex for some students who struggle. Which of the following would be most effective to support these students?

    A. Have struggling students take home extra reading for homework.

    B. Have students use silent sustained reading in class.

    C. Use a variety of leveled text and differentiate instruction based on needs.

    D. Have the reading coach come in and teach the class.

SOLUTION

When it comes to content area literacy, answer C has all the good words you should look for in the answer choices—*variety of levels, differentiated instruction, based on needs*. Extra homework and silent sustained reading are usually not the best answer choices. Having the reading coach teach your class is also not the most effective approach.

Correct Answer: C

1. Which of the following activities would be most appropriate in developing metacognition in students?
    A. Partner fluency reading
    B. Sight word memorization
    C. Essay writing
    D. Read aloud/think aloud

2. If a student is reading with automaticity, the student is:
    A. Reading through the text, only stopping at words he or she needs to decode.
    B. Reading with inflection and expression.
    C. Reading effortlessly through the text at >95% accuracy.
    D. Reading through the text using sight words.

3. A teacher provides the following feedback about her student's fluency.

    James read at approximately 125 WPM at the end of the school year. He is able to sound out unfamiliar words and makes few mistakes while reading. He does not skip words and has good word recognition.

    Which of the following should be added to the feedback to provide a comprehensive overview of the student's fluency?
    A. Rate
    B. Prosody
    C. Accuracy
    D. Automaticity

4. A student in Mrs. Black's class understands vocabulary and is a fluent reader; however, the student has difficulty with comprehension. What is the most effective instructional approach Mrs. Black can take to improve the student's comprehension?
    A. Question generation
    B. Timed reading
    C. Repeated reading
    D. Sight word memorization

5. Students have been working on a social science unit for some time. The teacher wants to increase students' critical thinking about certain topics within the unit. What would be the most effective approach?
    A. Have students work in their literature circles to evaluate text, present their claims and ideas, and find areas in the text that support those claims and ideas.
    B. Have students read a piece of text, debate the sides of the topic, and determine a winner of the debate.
    C. Have students work in collaborative groups, read a selection of text, and answer comprehension questions at the end of the text.
    D. Have students pick a topic presented in the unit, use the internet to research that topic, and write a detailed essay about the topic.

6. Which of the following conditions does fluency strengthen for better reading comprehension?

    A. Phonemic awareness

    B. Phonics

    C. Phonological awareness

    D. Cognitive endurance

7. A teacher wants to strengthen students' comprehension and critical thinking skills. Which of the following is the most effective way to do that?

    A. Paired reading to identify key words.

    B. Whole-group instruction to categorize vocabulary.

    C. Literature circles to analyze text.

    D. Chunking to break up difficult paragraphs

8. Before reading social science text, students look over the headings, charts, and graphs. They turn the headings of the text into questions. Then they read, summarize, and reread anything confusing or needing clarification. The students are engaging in:

    A. QAR

    B. SQ3R

    C. Literature circles

    D. Popcorn reading

9. Which of the following is the best activity for increasing reading comprehension?

    A. Decode difficult words

    B. Predict what will happen next

    C. Memorize sight words

    D. Read with expression

10. Teachers arrange students in groups. Each group reads and analyzes a piece of a text. Group members then join with members of other groups, and each student shares and discusses his or her section of the text. As the group shares, the entire text is covered. This activity is called:

    A. Think-pair-share

    B. Paired reading

    C. Guided reading

    D. Jigsaw

Competency 8 | Practice Problems Answer Explanations

Number	Answer	Explanation
1.	D	Metacognition is thinking about the process of thinking. Even if you did not know that definition, you probably know that cognition has to do with thinking. The only answer choice with the word think in it is answer D—read aloud/***think*** aloud. In this activity, the teacher models the reading thought process as the teacher reads aloud. The teacher shows how to figure out confusing words, derive meaning and move through the text by modeling the thought process taking place.
2.	C	Automaticity means the student is automatically recognizing words and moving through the text effortlessly. Answer A indicates the student is decoding words, which is the opposite of automaticity. Answer B describe prosody not automaticity. Answer D is not related.
3.	B	In this scenario, three things are described: rate in words per minute (wpm), accuracy (makes few mistakes), and automaticity (good word recognition). The only thing missing is how prosody, reading with inflection.
4.	A	Comprehension involves higher-order, critical thinking. It also requires metacognition. Question generation is a higher-order skill that aids in comprehension. Answers B, C, and D all support fluency not comprehension.
5.	A	Remember Bloom's Taxonomy when you see questions about critical thinking. All of these answer choices are good activities. However, there is only one with critical thinking elements in it—evaluating text and supporting claims using evidence. Answer A is the best choice.
6.	D	Fluency supports cognitive endurance. When students have the cognitive endurance to read through large sections of text and build meaning from that text. Students are not wasting cognitive energy on decoding words. Instead, students are reading fluently, using their cognitive energy towards comprehension and critical thinking, not word recognition and meaning.
7.	C	The key words in the question stem are *critical thinking*. When you see critical thinking in the question, looks for the corresponding Bloom's Taxonomy words in the answer choices. In this case, analyze is a high level, critical thinking skill. Therefore, C is the correct answer.
8.	B	This activity is SQ3R. S – Survey the headings, bold words, graphs, and charts. Q – Turn headings into questions 3R – Read, recite, repeat.
9.	B	Predicating is a comprehension activity. To predict, students must have comprehension of the story. Decoding difficult words and memorizing sight words support fluency. Reading with expression is prosody.
10.	D	Jigsaw is a cooperative learning activity in which each student or groups of students read and analyze a small piece of information that is part of a much larger piece. They then share what they learned with the class.

This page intentionally left blank.

Competency 9 | Knowledge of oral and written language acquisition and beginning reading

1. Evaluate and select approaches for involving stakeholders in reading initiatives for diverse learners.

2. Evaluate and select approaches to increase caregiver involvement in reading education.

3. Interpret reading policies, program information, and assessment data for the purpose of dissemination among stakeholders.

4. Select and evaluate instructional materials for comprehensive reading programs and reading intervention programs for diverse learners.

5. Identify criteria to determine the effectiveness of reading programs.

6. Interpret school data and program evaluation results to modify and improve curriculum content and instruction through professional learning.

7. Determine effective methods for coaching and supporting paraprofessionals, tutors, and volunteers to assist in reading instruction for diverse learners.

1. Evaluate and select approaches for involving stakeholders in reading initiatives for diverse learners.

In education, **stakeholders** are people who are invested in the success of the school and its students. Students, parents, teachers, administrators, community members, and business owners are all stakeholders. Typically, principals and assistant principals communicate initiatives or policies to community members and business owners. However, teachers must communicate with students and parents. The following example is how this might be presented on the FTCE Reading K-12 Test.

Example 1 Involving stakeholders

A teacher is implementing a new reading program in class. The teacher wants to involve parents and caregivers so they can participate in the new program. What is the most effective way to involve parents and caregivers?

    A. Send an email informing parents and caregivers about the new program and provide a link to online resources parents and caregivers can use at home.

    B. Have students tell their parents about the program and have parents sign a participation contract committing to at-home practice.

    C. Keep an up-to-date classroom website with reading strategies and resources available on the site for parents to use at home.

    D. Invite parents to a reading night to go over best practices and ways to implement reading at home and provide parents with resources to take home.

SOLUTION

Answer D has all the good elements for this situation: face-to-face interaction with parents, training on best practices, and resources to use at home. Answers A, B and C are incorrect because of two reasons. First, they all involve computers or internet, and not every family has access to computers or internet at home. Second, they do not help to train nor educate stakeholders on best practices.

Correct Answer: D

THINK ABOUT IT:

Teachers must consider cultural diversity when communicating with stakeholders. Because many families speak languages other than English, teachers must remember to send important information home in the native language. Also, not every student has access to the internet or email. Therefore, providing a hard copy written in students' native languages is the most effective way to communicate upcoming events, classroom expectations, and other important information with families.

2. Evaluate and select approaches to increase caregiver involvement in reading education.

When reading is reinforced at home, students are exposed to more text, more vocabulary, and more opportunities to achieve in reading. For example, caregivers can support children's vocabulary development by making connections between the story and children's personal experiences, as well as labeling, defining, and describing words. However, parents and caregivers may not know how to implement these strategies. Teachers should always encourage reading at home and even provide specific guidance for caregivers.

According to Gibbs, Lin, and Reed (2019), there are four key components drawn from research that are easy for caregivers to implement when reading with their children. The acronym IDEA stands for identify story elements, define unknown words, elicit inferential and literal information, and analyze illustrations. The following is an example of how this might look on the FTCE Reading K-12 Test.

Example 1 Reading at home

Which of the following activities would be most effective for parents to do at home with students?

    A. Encourage caregivers to require their children to read 20 min every night and provide rewards to children who finish.

    B. Have caregivers and students sign an at-home reading contract and revisit the contract periodically throughout the year.

    C. Encourage caregivers to use strategies when reading at home, such as identifying story elements and defining unknown words.

    D. Have the principal write a letter to parents explaining all students are required to read at home.

SOLUTION

The most effective approach is answer C because this method is specific and focuses on the skills. Answers A, B and D all use extrinsic rewards, contracts, and punitive measures which don't necessarily work.

Correct Answer: C

3. Interpret reading policies, program information, and assessment data for the purpose of dissemination among stakeholders.

On the FTCE Reading K-12 Test, you will be required to identify effective ways to communicate achievement results, in the form of qualitative and quantitative data, to all stakeholders.

Student assessment data from state testing is most often the type of data communicated to stakeholders. Therefore, it is important teachers understand how the state determines students' achievement levels.

According to the Florida Department of Education (2018), student performance on Florida's statewide assessments is categorized into five achievement levels. The following table provides information regarding student performance at each achievement level; this information is provided on student reports so that students, parents, and educators may interpret student results in a meaningful way.

Level 1	Level 2	Level 3	Level 4	Level 5
Inadequate	Below Satisfactory	Satisfactory	Proficient	Mastery
Highly likely to need substantial support for the next grade	Likely to need substantial support for the next grade	May need additional support for the next grade	Likely to excel in the next grade	Highly likely to excel in the next grade

▶ **Raw Score**

This is the number of questions a student gets correct on the exam. Raw scores are helpful in determining specific academic strengths and weaknesses.

▶ **Scale Score**

This is a linear transformation to indicate how a student faired on the test overall. Scaled scores are used to create a base scale for equating purposes. For example, if you score 67 out of 75 questions correctly on the ACT English exam, your scale score is a 31. Scale scores are effective for a general understanding of student achievement. However, they are not effective in determining specific student needs.

▶ **Percentile Rank**

A percentile rank tells how well a student performed in comparison to other students who took the same test. The percentile rank value is the percent of students the test taker scored better than on the assessment. A percentile rank of 73 means the student scored at or better than 73% of all the students who took the assessment. The percentile rank does not reflect how well an individual student scored or what they know. It simply compares a student to a much larger group of students to see how their performances compare.

▶ **Percentage**

A percentage is based out of 100 and can translate into how many problems a student answered or did not answer correctly. Although percentages and percentile rank both reference percents, they measure very different outcomes.

▶ **Stanine**

A stanine is a scaled score that is based on a nine-point scale. This simplified scale is a way to easily group students from the lowest performers to the top performers. Stanines are another way to compare groups of students, such as percentile ranks and other types of scaled scores.

QUICK TIP:

Typically, communication between the teacher and stakeholders comes in the form of parent-teacher conferences or student-led conferences. During these conferences teachers, parents, and students evaluate achievement results, qualitative data, and quantitative data to work together to map a plan for success.

4. **Select and evaluate instructional materials for comprehensive reading programs and reading intervention programs for diverse learners.**

Whenever selecting instructional materials or curriculum, teachers must consult the state-adopted standards. All instructional materials must be aligned to the standards. The next thing to consider is the research that supports using the instructional materials. Research-based strategies and instructional materials are those that have been effective in increasing student achievement in reading. That means there is a study or multiple studies that show using the instructional approach, material or strategy does, in fact, help students. The following is how this might look on the FTCE Reading K-12 Test.

Example 1 Selecting instructional materials

Which of the following would be most valuable when making a decision on whether to continue using a reading program?

    A. Summative assessment data

    B. Student survey data

    C. Parent survey data

    D. Classroom observation

SOLUTION

The question is asking what would be most beneficial to decide whether to continue the program. That means the teacher must determine if the program is working. Summative data will show that most effectively. Surveys will measure attitudes but not achievement. Classroom observations will show if a teacher is implementing the program but not if the program is working.

Correct Answer: A

5. **Identify criteria to determine the effectiveness of reading programs.**

This subskill of Competency 9 is an extension of the previous subskill—select and evaluate instructional materials for comprehensive reading programs and reading intervention programs for diverse learners. However, in this subskill, the teacher is required to determine if the program is effective. The only way to do that is to look at data to make decisions. This can be quantitative or qualitative data from multiple sources— formative and summative assessments. The following is how this might be presented on the FTCE Reading K-12 Test.

Example 1 Selecting effective materials

Which of the following would be most valuable to measure student and parent attitudes about the current reading program?

    A. Summative assessment data

    B. Survey data

    C. Norm-referenced test

    D. Classroom observation

SOLUTION

To measure attitudes about a program, use a survey. None of the other answer choices will yield qualitative data about attitudes. Student attitudes are important and should be considered—along with standards alignment, critical thinking and effectiveness—when evaluating a program.

Correct Answer: B

6. **Interpret school data and program evaluation results to modify and improve curriculum content and instruction through professional learning.**

Collaboration with colleagues is essential in becoming an effective teacher. Most schools have organized department meetings or team meetings. This collaboration is often referred to as professional learning communities (PLCs). When teachers work together to analyze data and design lessons to meet the needs of all students, they continuously improve instruction and increase student achievement. The most effective way to collaborate is through action research.

Action research

Action research is when teachers continuously collect both formative and summative data and use that data to differentiate instruction. This is ongoing, and part of the teachers' everyday practice. Most of the time, action research takes place in professional learning communities (PLCs) or department/grade-level teams. The following is an example scenario of effective action research.

Example 1 Effective action research

Science teachers at LMDS High School are working together to develop common assessments they will give their students throughout the semester. The assessments are aligned to the state standards and will serve as benchmark tests to measure student understanding of science concepts. The teachers meet once a week to go over assessment data and determine how to move forward with differentiated instruction. The teachers regularly engage in this action research.

The previous scenario is an example of teachers collaborating to evaluate outcomes (using data), adjusting planning based on the data (data-driven decision making), and continuously improving and reflecting on their practice. The following is an example of how this might be presented on the exam.

Which of the following is most effective in planning instruction for struggling learners?

    A. Attend professional development.

    B. Attend faculty meetings.

    C. Engage in action research.

    D. Survey students.

SOLUTION

Action research is data-driven decision making. If you see the term action research in an answer choice, it is the correct answer. Again, this competency is focused on making data-driven decisions.

Correct Answer: C

7. **Determine effective methods for coaching and supporting paraprofessionals, tutors, and volunteers to assist in reading instruction for diverse learners.**

Having a paraprofessional or volunteer in the classroom is an opportunity to provide even more support to students. It is important to remember; volunteers and paraprofessionals should always support the learning. They should be an extension of your instruction and help to enhance students' learning experiences. Below are some dos and don'ts to follow when working with paraprofessionals and volunteers.

Dos	Don'ts
Clarify roles and responsibilities of the teacher and of the paraprofessional or volunteer.	Decide last minute how to use paraprofessionals and volunteers when they come to the classroom.
Use paraprofessionals' and volunteers' strengths to enhance classroom instruction	Have paraprofessionals grade papers and complete administrative tasks.
Decrease an overreliance on the paraprofessional or volunteer.	Increase overreliance on the paraprofessional or volunteer.

The following is a way that this might be presented on the FTCE reading K-12 Test.

Example 1 Role of the paraprofessional

At the end of the semester, a teacher meets with a paraprofessional who helps students who are ELL. The teacher and the paraprofessional discuss a plan to increase independent learning, decrease an over reliance on the paraprofessional, and scaffold when necessary. Which of the following represents this meeting between the teacher and paraprofessional?

    A. Interim reading goal meeting

    B. Specially designed instruction

    C. Specific intervention strategies

    D. Clarifying roles and responsibilities

SOLUTION

The teacher and the paraprofessional are defining new roles for the paraprofessional. The teacher wants to decrease the amount of dependence the ELL students have on the paraprofessional. Therefore, it is important to define roles and responsibilities moving forward. In addition, clarifying roles and responsibilities is part of the Dos in working with paraprofessionals and volunteers. You might be tempted to choose specific intervention strategies. However, in the question stem, it specifically says the teacher wants to increase independence and decrease dependence on the paraprofessional.

Correct Answer: D

Competency 9 | Practice Problems

1. A teacher will be using a new reading program in class. What would be the most effective way to disseminate information about the program to parents and stakeholders?

    A. Send home information to parents from the company's website explaining the program.

    B. Present research and evidence supporting the program and a plan to monitor progress.

    C. Show parents a survey where students expressed interest in the program.

    D. Explain that the district expects everyone to participate in the program.

2. Use the information below to answer the following question.

Student A's 3rd grade fluency measure		
Beginning of school year	Middle of school year	End of school year
70wpm	90wpm	115wpm

Standard fluency measures for 3rd grade		
Beginning of school year	Middle of school year	End of school year
85wpm	105wpm	125wpm

A 3rd grade teacher is preparing for a parent/teacher conference. The teacher is looking over student data and comparing it to the standard. What should this teacher communicate to parents based on the data above?

    A. Student A is on track and exceeding grade-level expectations.

    B. Student A is on track and meeting grade-level expectations.

    C. Student A is behind but approaching grade-level expectations.

    D. Student A is behind and receding in grade-level expectations.

3. A paraprofessional is working with a 4th grade reading teacher. The teacher plans to implement a whole group reading activity. What can the paraprofessional do to assist the teacher in instruction?

    A. Walk around the room and assist the students and teacher when needed.

    B. Break students up into small groups and re-teach concepts.

    C. Grade papers and finish up other administrative tasks for the teacher.

    D. Monitor student behavior and address disruptions.

4. Which of the following should be considered first when choosing text for a reading program?

    A. Is the text interesting?

    B. Does the text increase critical thinking?

    C. Is the text aligned to the state standards?

    D. Is the text above grade level?

5. A principal wants to assess a teacher's reading program. What is most effective approach she can take to determine the effectiveness of the reading program?

   A. The principal can observe the teacher's class.

   B. The principal can see if the program's objectives were met.

   C. The teacher can write a reflection about the reading program and turn it in to the principal.

   D. The principal can ask the students to evaluate the program and the teacher.

6. Which of the following ways is most effective when encouraging caregivers to engage in at-home reading exercises with students?

   A. Have caregivers document pages read per night in a reading log.

   B. Have caregivers provide rewards when students read at home.

   C. Provide caregivers with a set of questions to answer after reading.

   D. Provide caregivers with suggested reading activities for at-home reading.

7. Students are engaged and motivated to read when these elements align: home, community, and school but only when the school:

   A. has concrete rules for reading.

   B. focuses on students' reading scores.

   C. focuses on including all stakeholders in reading programs.

   D. has a clear rewards system for students who participate in reading programs.

8. Which of the following is most effective in increasing parent involvement in children's reading?

   A. Have students and parents pick out reading books together.

   B. Have students summarize lessons from school to their parents.

   C. Have students and parents sign a reading contract.

   D. Go over school grade data with parents.

9. Which of the following approaches is most effective in determining if teachers should continue using a reading program?

   A. Measure outcomes at the end of the semester and determine if there was sufficient growth.

   B. Survey students to see if they thought the reading program was interesting.

   C. Ask the department head and team leader if they will continue to use the program.

   D. Ask the principal to come in and observe and determine if the program works.

10. Use the data below to answer the following question.

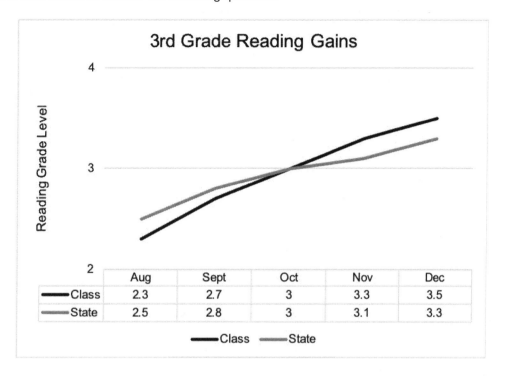

3rd Grade Reading Gains

	Aug	Sept	Oct	Nov	Dec
Class	2.3	2.7	3	3.3	3.5
State	2.5	2.8	3	3.1	3.3

A teacher is evaluating a new reading program. The teacher compares the class data to the state data. Based on the data above, what would be the most effective decision?

A. Discontinue using the program and start a new program for second semester.

B. Introduce another program alongside the current program.

C. Split the class and use a different program for those falling behind.

D. Continue using the program and monitor progress for second semester.

This page intentionally left blank.

Number	Answer	Explanation
1.	B	The most effective way to communicate decisions in the classroom is to present evidence or research that supports those decisions. Answer B also has all the good words seen in correct answer choices.
2.	C	The student is making gains but is still behind the state average or standard fluency measure. While the student is making gains, the student is not on track. On track means the student is meeting the standard. The student is approaching. Therefore, the teacher should continue the interventions and programs because they are working.
3.	A	Because this is a whole-group activity, the most appropriate thing for the paraprofessional to do is support the students and the teacher when needed. Breaking students up goes against the whole group activity. Grading papers is never the correct answer. Monitoring student behavior is a punitive approach. The paraprofessional is most productive in answer choice A.
4.	C	First, always align decisions to standards. Books, curriculum, and materials should all be aligned to the standards before they can even be considered for the classroom. Once alignment is established, then the teacher should consider critical thinking, interest and grade-level.
5.	B	Objectives are the skills and behaviors students will display after using the program. Measuring if the objectives were met is the most effective way to determine if the program was successful. Observing the class will not tell the principal if the program is working. Writing a reflection and asking students to evaluate the teacher is not as effective as measuring objectives.
6.	D	Caregivers may not have any idea how to approach reading at home with students. Therefore, providing suggested activities is most effective here. Having caregivers document number of pages read or answering questions is laborious and not effective, eliminating answers A and C. Extrinsic rewards are usually never the answer in reading instruction, eliminating answer B.
7.	C	The term *all stakeholders* is a good term. When the school is focused on including all stakeholders, the school is focused on students, parents and community. All the other answer choices are punitive, focused on extrinsic rewards, and not appropriate.
8.	A	Picking out reading books together is an authentic and inclusive way to promote reading at home.
9.	A	The only way to determine if the program was successful in increasing students reading skills is to measure reading outcomes. None of the other answer choices will tell the teacher if the program was effective in increasing reading skills.
10.	D	The program is working because the class went from below the state to exceeding the state. Therefore, the teacher should continue the program and monitor progress to see if it is still working second semester. Also, the term *monitor progress* is a on the good words list.

This page intentionally left blank.

1. What should a teacher consider before using a particular piece of research?

    A. Is the research easy to understand?

    B. Is the research relevant?

    C. Is the research used by other teachers?

    D. Is the research easily communicated?

2. A teacher is looking over recent reading research and determining if it is reliable. Which of the following questions should the teacher ask to determine if the research is reliable?

    A. Is the study testing what it intends to test?

    B. Did the study yield consistent results in multiple administrations?

    C. Was the study conducted by a private company or organization?

    D. Were there enough people who participated in the study?

3. Which of the following classroom scenarios outlines Vygotsky's Zone of Proximal Development?

    A. Students are reading silently on their own.

    B. Students are using a KWL chart to activate prior knowledge.

    C. Students are working in groups to evaluate text.

    D. Students are using whole language to learn how to read.

4. If a study has internal validity but not external validity, what can be said about the study?

    A. The study was conducted properly, but the results cannot necessarily be applied to the real world.

    B. The study was not conducted properly, and the results cannot necessarily be applied to the real world.

    C. The study was conducted properly, and the results can be applied to the real world.

    D. The study was not conducted properly, and the results cannot be applied to the real world.

5. Which of the following activity follows Piaget's stages of cognitive development?

    A. Students are filling out a worksheet.

    B. Students are working in groups.

    C. Students are following procedures.

    D. Students are activating schema before they read.

6. Which of the following theorists believed children have an innate sense of reading?

    A. Noam Chomsky

    B. Lev Vygotsky

    C. Jean Piaget

    D. Louise Rosenblatt

7. The theory that learning should be relevant to students' lives and that students should interact with their learning is:

   A. Behaviorism

   B. Stages of cognitive development

   C. Constructivism

   D. Zone of Proximal Development

8. Which of the following approaches would be considered a bottom up method?

   A. Students are reading in groups and discussing text.

   B. Students are reading silently on their own.

   C. Students are working in centers.

   D. Students are practicing phonics.

9. Where can a teacher find reliable and valid research to apply in the reading classroom?

   A. An education blog

   B. An academic journal

   C. The department head

   D. The district library

10. What can a teacher look over to determine if research is scholarly?

    A. The bibliography

    B. The authors

    C. The number of pages

    D. The date

11. If a study's results can be applied to the outside world, the study has:

    A. Accuracy

    B. Timeliness

    C. Internal validity

    D. External validity

12. Students are using their reading response journals to interact with text. What theorist does this activity align to?

    A. Noam Chomsky

    B. Lev Vygotsky

    C. Louise Rosenblatt

    D. Jean Piaget

13. Use the passage below to answer the following question.

Hippos, although cute, are aggressive. They have been known to attack villagers who fish in the rivers inhabited by hippos. In fact, in the last 2 years, there have been 150 hippo attacks across Africa.

What type of text structure is the author of the above passage using?

   A. Cause and effect

   B. Main idea and details

   C. Chronological

   D. Problem/Solution

14. Use the passage below to answer the following question.

When Jade was younger, she always thought she would be a star, and now she was so close she could taste it. However, her rival, Sarah, had already devised a plan to unravel all of Jade's hard work. Sarah was proud that she had concocted such an air-tight plan.

What type of text structure is the author using?

   A. First person

   B. Second Person

   C. Third person objective

   D. Third person omniscient

15. A teacher is working on literacy in her social science classroom. She wants students to have a comprehensive understanding of the topics. What would be the best approach to accomplish this?

   A. Have students work in groups to read the textbook.

   B. Have students choose novels based on their interests

   C. Have students read individually and answer comprehension questions.

   D. Use a balanced literacy program rich with informational and literary text.

16. This type of text describes one's own life:

   A. Autobiography

   B. Biography

   C. Historical fiction

   D. Expository nonfiction

17. Which of the following should a teacher consider when choosing multicultural text?

   A. Will the students understand the text?

   B. Will the students be interested in the text?

   C. Are there diverse characters in heroic or powerful roles in the text?

   D. Did students get parent permission before reading the text?

18. If a teacher is considering the presentation of issues in multicultural texts, what should the teacher consider before presenting these issues?

    A. If issues are too graphic for young readers

    B. If the district has approved the text and its content

    C. If the issues presented are accurate and appropriate

    D. If the issues presented are interesting and engaging

19. What should a teacher consider first when choosing texts for a unit on Earth Space science?

    A. Is the text on grade level?

    B. Are the students interested in the topics presented in the text?

    C. Is the text aligned to the state-adopted standards?

    D. Did the science department head approve the text?

20. A teacher is observing students as they read to see how they interact with text. She will use this information to determine what text to use moving forward. The teacher is using what measure of text complexity?

    A. Qualitative

    B. Quantitative

    C. Qualitative and quantitative

    D. Rubric

21. A student struggles with grade-level text but wants to get better at her reading. What approach would be most effective when choosing text for this student?

    A. Choose books the student is interested in.

    B. Give the student rewards when she finishes grade-level text.

    C. Encourage the student to practice with text on her reading level.

    D. Encourage the student to above grade-level text so she can catch up.

22. Which of the following would be most beneficial for a teacher to use if the teacher wants to expose students to different genres of text?

    A. A classroom library

    B. Textbooks

    C. Novels

    D. Poetry books

23. Which of the following would be helpful when exposing students to syllables in poetry?

    A. Haiku

    B. Epic

    C. Myth

    D. Sonnet

24. A Lexile is a type of:

    A. Standardized test

    B. Text leveling system

    C. Genre

    D. Poem

25. What would be the most effective way for a teacher to use a diagnostic assessment?

    A. Compare students

    B. Monitor progress

    C. Measure skills application

    D. Determine prior knowledge

26. A student is taking the English Language Arts Florida Standards Assessment. What type of assessment is the student taking?

    A. Formative

    B. Performance-based

    C. Norm-reference

    D. Criterion-reference

27. A teacher is planning a science unit. She has struggling readers in the class, and some of the science text is complex. Which of the following is the most effective approach to take to help all students with the material?

    A. Administer a diagnostic assessment to measure baseline skills, then use a variety of formative assessments to monitor progress and make decisions.

    B. Administer a criterion-referenced assessment to see what skills students are lacking, then use a summative to measure success.

    C. Administer a norm-referenced assessment to rank and compare students' skills, then group students and use a summative at the end of learning.

    D. Administer a summative at the beginning of the lesson, then use a criterion-referenced assessment to measure standards.

28. Which of the following assessments should a teacher use to measure outcomes at the end of a semester?

    A. Norm-referenced

    B. Diagnostic

    C. Summative

    D. Formative

29. A teacher is assessing story sequence. The teacher has several ELL students who are not yet fluent in writing in English. What is the most effective way to assess students' skill in sequence while keeping the ELL students in mind?

    A. Use a paraprofessional to help the student write in English.

    B. Use an oral assessment to measure skills.

    C. Use Spanish to English worksheets on story sequence.

    D. Require students to write in English.

30. If a teacher wants to measure students' skills over the course of a semester, what would be the most effective approach?

    A. Use a variety of formal and informal assessments.

    B. Use a variety of assessments and rewards.

    C. Use a variety of performance-based assessments.

    D. Use a variety of norm-referenced and criterion referenced assessments.

31. Students will be completing a research project over the course of a few weeks. Which of the following approaches is most effective?

    A. Provide students with a rubric to convey expectations and scoring criteria.

    B. Allow students to use the computer lab as much as possible to conduct research.

    C. Have students work in cooperative groups to discuss ideas and research topics.

    D. Send information home to parents so they understand what is expected for the project.

32. A teacher is having a student read aloud for one minute. As the student reads, the teacher notes any miscues. What type of assessment is this?

    A. Informal reading inventory

    B. Performance-based

    C. Running record

    D. Informal writing task

33. After reading a leveled passage, the teacher asks a student follow-up questions assessing comprehension and recall. What type of assessment is this?

    A. Performance-based

    B. Summative

    C. Oral fluency assessment

    D. Informal reading inventory (IRI)

34. Which of the following is the most effective way to use a diagnostic assessment?

    A. To group students

    B. To make decisions

    C. To rank students

    D. To follow up

35. A student scores a level 3 on the English Language Arts Florida Standards Assessments. What type of instruction should this student receive?

    A. The student needs substantial support and interventions to meet grade-level expectations

    B. The student needs additional support to maintain grade-level expectations.

    C. The student does not need any support because the student is proficient.

    D. The student needs individual support from the reading coach.

36. Which of the following is one measure of students' reading levels?

    A. Have students sequence the story.

    B. Evaluate students' writing.

    C. Calculate how many words per min students read.

    D. Observe students working in groups.

37. Which of the following activities is most effective for motivating ELL students in reading?

    A. Encourage safe times to use academic language and reading aloud.

    B. Have students work in cooperative groups and change groups regularly.

    C. Work individually with ELL students on fluency and comprehension.

    D. Group ELL students together to work with the paraprofessional.

38. After looking over students' writing, a teacher notices 5 students are struggling with the same skill. What should the teacher do?

    A. Use a whole-group instructional approach to address the concepts before the next lesson.

    B. Use a whole-group graphic organizer activity to reinforce the skill.

    C. Use a small-group heterogeneous group with peer-tutors.

    D. Use a small-group homogeneous group temporarily to apply interventions.

39. The teacher is having students read from text. While reading, they stop to generate questions and discuss. What technique are the teacher and students using?

    A. SQ3R

    B. QAR

    C. KWL

    D. Basal

40. Which of the following is the most effective way to motivate students to read?

    A. Provide students with incentives for completing reading logs.

    B. Build an information rich classroom library.

    C. Allow students to work in groups when they read.

    D. Call home to parents with positive reading progress.

41. Which of the following would be considered intrinsic motivators for student reading?

    A. Calling home to communicate reading gains with parents.

    B. Allowing for extra time at the end of class if students complete their reading.

    C. Going over reading data and setting weekly and monthly goals.

    D. Having the principal come in and congratulate students on their reading progress.

42. A teacher is allowing students to show mastery of skills by building a brochure, recording a podcast, writing an essay, or conducting a performance. The teacher is:

    A. Considering students learning preferences

    B. Making learning fun and interesting

    C. Considering students low reading levels

    D. Allowing for a rewards

43. Teachers in the reading department are working together to develop grouping practices for the next semester. Which of the following would be most effective?

    A. Look over reading data and plan for interventions.

    B. Keep students in homogeneous groups for the rest of the semester.

    C. Group students by behavior.

    D. Group students by interest.

44. Which of the following would be the most effective way to help ELL students apply speaking and listening skills?

    A. State reading test

    B. Silent sustained reading

    C. Repeated reading

    D. Role play

45. Which of the following would be the most effective way to use Basal Reading for struggling readers?

    A. Independent reading

    B. Repeated reading

    C. Read alouds

    D. Vocabulary exercises

46. Which of the following is not a component of intrinsic motivation?

    A. Autonomy

    B. Relatedness

    C. Anonymity

    D. Competence

47. Which of the following is most effective for moving students in and out of flexible grouping?

    A. Rewards for effective transitions

    B. Stay in groups as long as possible

    C. Practiced procedures

    D. Group students by behavior

48. Which of the following would be most effective in motivating students to self-govern their reading groups in a way that increases their understanding of text?

    A. Allow students to choose what they learn.

    B. Give students extra social time when they master skills.

    C. Set clear consequences for bad behavior.

    D. Make the reading activities and the text related to the real-world.

49. Use the picture to answer the following question.

    Students see the following image and say, "Frog!" What stage of word recognition are the students in?

    A. Pre-alphabetic

    B. Partial alphabetic

    C. Full-alphabetic

    D. Consolidated alphabetic

50. These are the smallest units of meanings in words.

    A. Phonemes

    B. Morphemes

    C. Semantics

    D. Phonics

51. A teacher is helping students with their speaking and listening skills. Which of the following oral language element is she focusing on?

    A. Discourse

    B. Phonology

    C. Morphology

    D. Phonics

52. Which of the following activities focuses on morphology?

   A.   Breaking words apart by individual sounds

   B.   Using blends to combine consonants

   C.   Analyzing prefixes, suffixes, and roots

   D.   Following grammar rules

53. This is an overarching skill that includes identifying and manipulating units of oral language, including parts of words, syllables, onsets, and rimes.

   A.   Phonemic awareness

   B.   Vocabulary awareness

   C.   Structural awareness

   D.   Phonological Awareness

54. Which of the following is an example of semantic cueing?

   A.   Have students use phonics to figure out difficult words.

   B.   Have students use spelling to figure out difficult words.

   C.   Have students use grammar to figure out difficult words.

   D.   Have students use meaning to figure out difficult words.

55. A teacher is working with students on a phonemic awareness activity. This activity is mostly:

   A.   Visual

   B.   Kinesthetic

   C.   Auditory

   D.   Read/write

56. Which of the following would be the best activity for phonics instruction?

   A.   Complete a spelling worksheet.

   B.   Use flashcards to memorize sight words.

   C.   Focus on why vowel sounds are long in some words.

   D.   Determine how many sounds are in different words.

57. Students are breaking up the following word below by:

   d/e/s/c/r/i/b/e

   A.   Syllables

   B.   Phonemes

   C.   Semenatics

   D.   Morphemes

58. The student uses the following picture to say the word ball. What stage of word recognition is the student in?

B

A. Pre-alphabetic

B. Partial alphabetic

C. Full-alphabetic

D. Consolidated alphabetic

59. This is when students combine their knowledge of word recognition to decipher large units of words and phrases.

A. Pre-alphabetic

B. Partial alphabetic

C. Full-alphabetic

D. Consolidated alphabetic

60. During a guided reading activity of informational text, the teacher focuses on the structure of different words, using prefixes, suffixes, and roots. The teacher is helping students use what cognitive working system?

A. Semantic

B. Graphophonic

C. Lexile

D. Syntactic

61. Which of the following list of words would be most appropriate for a lesson morphology?

A. fix, tricks, picks

B. irregular, irresponsible, irreplaceable

C. sleep, sheep, steep

D. place, put, shut

62. Students are using the tiles below. They use the first tile (tr) and match it with the others to make words.

The students are working on:

A.   syllables and rime

B.   onset and rime

C.   onset and segmentation

D.   deletion and rime

63. A teacher is working with students on words. She tells the students to say the word *hat*. They all say the word *hat*. Then she tells them to say the word hat with a /p/ sound in the beginning instead of the /h/ sound. The teacher and students are using what strategy?

A.   Substitution

B.   Deletion

C.   Segmenting

D.   Isolation

64. Based on the following instructional practices, what type of lesson is the teacher working on?

•   Teach students to break words down by individual sounds.

•   Teach students to focus on sounds as they rhyme words.

A.   Phonemic awareness

B.   Decoding

C.   Phonics

D.   Structural analysis

65. A student is struggling to read fluently because she is trying to sound out high frequency words. What can the teacher do to help this student?

A.   Have the student work with a buddy.

B.   Help the student write the words over and over again.

C.   Have the student use the words in an essay.

D.   Help the students to memorize sight words.

66. Which of the following is a CVCC word?

A.   Make

B.   Pat

C.   Tack

D.   Shack

67. A teacher is working with ELL students who are in the emergent stage of reading. What should the teacher focus on initially?

    A.   prioritize conducting read alouds and literature circle activities.

    B.   first teach sight word recognition and CVC word decoding skills.

    C.   first develop students' oral and academic vocabulary knowledge.

    D.   include assignments that involve working with stories and writing.

68. Which of the following activities would be most appropriate for students struggling with silent letter rules?

    A.   Read aloud/think aloud

    B.   Writing vocabulary words

    C.   Phonemic awareness exercises

    D.   Phonics exercises

69. Which of the following would be the most appropriate activity for a 1ˢᵗ grade lesson on syllables?

    A.   Decode two-syllable words

    B.   Clap two-syllable words

    C.   Write two-syllable words

    D.   Find two-syllable words in a dictionary

70. Students are saying simple words aloud. They say the word *bat*, then they say the word *at*. They say the word *pat* then say the word *at*. The students are using what strategy?

    A.   Deletion

    B.   Substitution

    C.   Blending

    D.   Isolation

71. Which of the following would be most appropriate for students memorizing sight words?

    A.   Write words over and over again

    B.   Play a memorization game

    C.   Decode words

    D.   Look words up in the dictionary

72. A few students are struggling with their *ou* sounds when they are reading. Which of the following would be the most appropriate approach to help these students?

    A.   Have students fill out a worksheet with *ou* words.

    B.   Conduct a whole-group session on digraphs.

    C.   Work in a small-group on vowel teams.

    D.   Have students work on *ou* sounds for homework.

73. Which of the following set of words would be most appropriate when practicing consonant blends?

    A.   Fuzz, fill, bass

    B.   Tack, back, sack

    C.   Dog, cat, tub

    D.   Brag, strap, slip

74. Which of the following words would be most appropriate to analyze in a phonics lesson?

    A.   Happy

    B.   Play

    C.   Bat

    D.   Receive

75. The teacher is having students break apart compound words and use prefixes, suffixes, and roots to determine meaning in words. The students and teacher are working on:

    A.   Segmenting

    B.   Blending

    C.   Morphology

    D.   Substituting

76. Which is NOT a best practice for vocabulary instruction?

    A.   Model using context clues

    B.   Teaching prefixes, suffixes, and roots

    C.   Explicit instruction using a dictionary

    D.   Using word walls for target vocabulary

77. A teacher is working with ELL students who are in the emergent stage of vocabulary acquisition. What should the teacher work on first?

    A.   Listen vocabulary

    B.   Reading vocabulary

    C.   Speaking vocabulary

    D.   Writing vocabulary

78. Which of the following is considered tier I vocabulary?

    A.   Academic specific words

    B.   Words that occur in students' textbooks

    C.   Word with the silent /ph/.

    D.   High frequency, everyday words

79. Which of the following is most effective when teaching academic vocabulary?

    A.   Use memorization games to remember words.

    B.   Use morphology to break down difficult words.

    C.   Use a glossary to copy down difficult words.

    D.   Use context from the content area to learn new words.

80. Which of the following activities would be most appropriate for ELL students learning conversational vocabulary?

    A.   Role play

    B.   Read alouds

    C.   Literature circles

    D.   Deletion exercises

81. Which activity is most appropriate for teaching multiple meaning words?

    A.   Structural analysis

    B.   Sight words

    C.   Contextual analysis

    D.   Phonic analysis

82. Which of the following activities is most effective when teaching ELL students to advance from tier I words to tier II words?

    A.   Have students analyze both common and applied definitions for new words.

    B.   Have students complete word lists for homework.

    C.   Have students memorize the tier II words.

    D.   Have students match common words to pictures.

83. Which of the following describes tier III words?

    A.   These words should be memorized because they occur in almost every text. These words do not always follow phonics rules.

    B.   These words occur across contexts. More common in writing and everyday speech, these words enhance comprehension of a text.

    C.   These words are used in everyday speech. These words are learned in conversation. They rarely require direct instruction.

    D.   These words often pertain to a specific content area. They are best learned within the content of the lesson or subject matter.

84. Which of the following skills combination represents expressive vocabulary?

    A.   Reading and writing

    B.   Reading and listening

    C.   Speaking and listening

    D.   Speaking and writing

85. Which of the following would be the most appropriate activity for students working on their receptive vocabulary?

    A.   Conduct a presentation.

    B.   Listen to a story on tape.

    C.   Discuss stories in literature circles.

    D.   Engage in a role play conversation.

86. Which of the following would be the most appropriate activity for students working on their expressive vocabulary?

    A.   Read a book.

    B.   Listen to a story on tape.

    C.   Discuss stories in literature circles.

    D.   Look up vocabulary words.

87. Which of the following words would be considered a tier II vocabulary word?

    A.   she

    B.   examined

    C.   lithosphere

    D.   place

88. Mrs. Smith is teaching a science lesson on cell growth. Nucleus, membrane, and lysosome are words being used to label the cell. These words are examples of what kind of vocabulary?

    A.   Tier II

    B.   Tier I

    C.   Tier III

    D.   Context vocabulary

89. Which of the following is most effective for a student who is struggling with a word in the textbook?

    A.   Look the word up in the glossary.

    B.   Use context clues.

    C.   Write the word down.

    D.   Skip the word.

90. Why is it important for students to work on fluency?

    A.   Fluency helps a student read quickly, which helps the student get through the reading with enough time to answer comprehension questions.

    B.   Fluency reduces the amount of time a student spends decoding words, which helps the student apply cognitive energy to understanding the text.

    C.   Fluency helps a student increase correct words per minute measures, which helps the teacher group students into comprehension centers.

    D.   Fluency allows the students to decode words more efficiently, which helps the student focus on complex vocabulary rather than sight words.

91. A student is reading with proper tone, stopping at punctuation, and reading fluently. The student is displaying:

    A. Decoding

    B. Prosody

    C. Tone

    D. Application

92. A student is struggling during reading. The student often stops when encountering high-frequency words and tries to decode them. This interrupts the reading and makes it difficult for the student to understand meaning in the text. Which of the following interventions should the teacher employ?

    A. The teacher should have the student focus on spelling because spelling is phonics, and phonics is a necessary part of the comprehension process.

    B. The teacher should have the student take a diagnostic test and then have the reading coach work with the student where the student's skills are weak.

    C. The teacher should use a running record to record the miscues a student demonstrates during one minute of reading.

    D. The teacher should focus on fluency and automaticity strategies for this student because proper fluency and automaticity will reduce the cognitive demand needed for decoding, leaving more cognitive space for comprehension.

93. When a teacher asks students to make predictions about a text, he or she is fostering the students':

    A. Fluency

    B. Comprehension

    C. Decoding skills

    D. Automaticity

94. Why is it important for a teacher to integrate oral, written, and visual elements from texts when teaching comprehension?

    A. Integrating oral, written, and visual elements from texts helps to make the material interesting to students, which helps students comprehend the text.

    B. Integrating oral, written, and visual elements from texts helps to make classical text modern so students can understand the text.

    C. Integrating oral, written, and visual elements from texts makes reading the text easier for students to understand than if those elements were not integrated.

    D. Integrating oral, written, and visual elements from texts enhances the meaning of complex text, which helps students comprehend the text.

95. A teacher is engaging in a running record with students individually. As the student reads, the teacher indicates, with a tally mark, any time a student makes a mistake in the reading. After one minute, the teacher stops the student, tallies the mistakes, and determines the student's words per minute. The teacher is measuring the student's:

   A. Accuracy and comprehension

   B. Fluency and comprehension

   C. Accuracy and rate

   D. Rate and prosody

96. Which of the following is a component of fluency?

   A. Reading comprehension

   B. Identifying text structure

   C. Summarizing events in a text

   D. Reading with prosody

97. The teacher is using a text where each chapter is written in first-person from a different character's perspective. What would be the benefit of using this novel?

   A. Students can analyze each character's perspective of events occurring in the text.

   B. Students can check to see if the narrator switches point of view anywhere in the text.

   C. Students can each read for the different characters in the text.

   D. Students can identify similarities among all the characters in the text.

98. Which of the following would be an effective activity to help students think and listen critically?

   A. Collaborative discussions where students evaluate what each other is saying and repeat pieces of those discussions back before presenting a new idea

   B. A debate where students use proper parliamentary procedures to state their opinions and cite evidence to support their opinions

   C. Literature circles where every student plays a role in the outcome of the discussion

   D. An activity where students work together to build a website

99. A teacher is asking students to compare two texts with similar themes and evaluate their meanings and how they relate to each other. This is an example of:

   A. Critical thinking

   B. Qualitative thinking

   C. Complexity of text

   D. Text to self

100. Several students in the class are struggling with comprehension skills. Which of the following would be most effective when helping these students?

   A. Partner reading to focus on key vocabulary words.

   B. Comprehension games for maximum engagement.

   C. Differentiated instruction with targeted interventions.

   D. Whole-group memorization strategies.

101. What can a science teacher do to ensure he is helping to develop reading comprehension?

   A. Provide opportunities for students to engage in content area reading.

   B. Provide opportunities for students to engage in content area writing.

   C. Use graphic organizers and other tools when reading in science.

   D. All of the above.

102. Which of the following activities involves critical thinking and higher-order skills?

   A. Students participate in cooperative learning to identify effective writing techniques.

   B. Students complete a worksheet where they label parts of a sentence.

   C. Students engage in writing workshops to evaluate and critique essays.

   D. Students pair up to read excerpts of a text.

103. Which of the following would be most effective in developing students' comprehension of complex text?

   A. Encourage students to memorize portions of the text.

   B. Encourage students to ask questions about the text.

   C. Encourage students to partner read the text.

   D. Encourage students to read the text for homework.

104. Which of the following activities would be effective in relating text to self?

   A. Jigsaw

   B. Think-pair-share

   C. Reading response journal

   D. Literature circles

105. A teacher is modeling the process of reading comprehension. The teacher uses context clues to figure out difficult words. The teacher stops to think aloud and predict, summarize, and ask questions. What skill is the teacher modeling?

   A. Metacognition

   B. Fluency

   C. Vocabulary

   D. Reading aloud

106. A teacher arranges students in groups. Each group member is assigned a different piece of information. Group members then join with members of other groups assigned the same piece of information, and research and/or share ideas about the information. Eventually, students return to their original groups as experts on the pieces they researched. Students then share the information and "piece together" a clear picture of the topic at hand. This activity is called:

   A. Chunking

   B. Jigsaw

   C. Blending

   D. Seminar

107. Which strategy would best help students develop the ability to synthesize reading material?

    A. Reading an informational passage and working in small groups to create semantic maps of the organizational patterns presented in the text

    B. Highlighting predetermined information (criteria) such as main idea, thesis statement, supporting details, and specialized vocabulary in a reading passage

    C. Reading two passages and brainstorming in small groups to create Venn diagrams that compare and contrast theme, content, characters, and details of the texts

    D. Rewriting a passage from a classic play, such as Shakespeare's *Othello* or *Romeo and Juliet*, in standard English and one other vernacular speech pattern

108. A teacher has students work in cooperative groups. They will read the text and then highlight the key points. They will then present the key points to the class. What are the students doing?

    A. Predicating

    B. Foreshadowing

    C. Generating questions

    D. Summarizing

109. What can a teacher do to ensure the paraprofessional in the classroom is being used most effectively?

    A. Meet with the paraprofessional periodically to plan instruction.

    B. Have the paraprofessional only work with ELL students.

    C. Have the paraprofessional grade papers so the teacher has more time to teach.

    D. Allow the paraprofessional to teach class when needed.

110. Based on the data below, which of the statements are accurate?

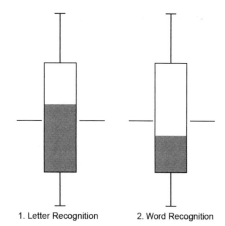

1. Letter Recognition   2. Word Recognition

    A. Students performed at or above proficiency in both word recognition and letter recognition.

    B. Students performed below proficiency in word recognition and letter recognition.

    C. Students performed at or above proficiency in word recognition; students performed below proficiency in letter recognition.

    D. Students performed at or above proficiency in letter recognition; students performed below proficiency in word recognition

111. Which of the following is most effective in communicating student goals and achievement to caregivers and parents?

    A. Report cards home

    B. Email to parents/guardian

    C. Student-led conferences

    D. Meetings with the principal

112. Teachers in the reading department use their professional learning community (PLC) time to analyze formative and summative data and evaluate what is working in the classroom. They then make decisions as a team for the next week's assignments and assessments. They meet again in two weeks and go over the data from the previous week and then identify what is working. This process is ongoing throughout the year. The teachers are engaging in:

    A. Planning assessments

    B. Action research

    C. Formative assessment teaching

    D. Departmental meetings

113. The district reading leadership team has evaluated data and determined that teachers must implement informal progress monitoring during instruction. Which of the following methods would support this district effort?

    A. Schedule team meetings with reading coaches.

    B. Provide professional development on formative assessments for all teachers.

    C. Purchase a formal assessment program for the district with training.

    D. Hire additional academic coaches to track the students' reading growth

114. If a teacher is planning a whole-group activity to start a lesson, what would be the best way to use the paraprofessional for the class?

    A. To observe students and help when needed

    B. To monitor behavior and manage the class

    C. To grade papers and take attendance

    D. To work 1-1 with students

115. Which of the following is most effective when communicating with a classroom volunteer?

    A. Rules and regulations

    B. Student test data

    C. Clear expectations and roles

    D. Faculty meeting schedule

116. Which of the following should be used to determine if a program was effective or not?

    A. Parent survey

    B. Student survey

    C. School Climate survey

    D. Student reading scores

117.   Which of the following would be most effective in involving parents in at-home reading?

    A.   Provide parents with suggested guidelines and activities.

    B.   Provide parents with a rubric and scoring sheet.

    C.   Have parents come in for a reading training.

    D.   Have students and parents sign reading contracts.

118.   Which of the following approaches is most effective in determining if teachers should continue using a reading program?

    A.   Measure outcomes at the end of the semester and determine if there was sufficient growth.

    B.   Survey students to see if they thought the reading program was interesting.

    C.   Ask the department head and team leader if they will continue to use the program.

    D.   Ask the principal to come in and observe and determine if the program works.

119.   Given the data, what should be the teacher's next step regarding this student?

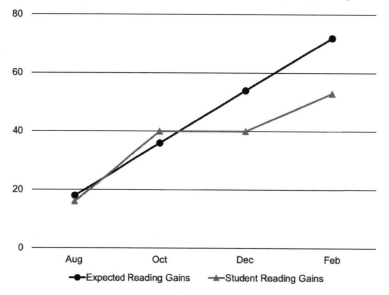

    A.   Continue with current reading instruction by using the district-mandated materials with fidelity because the student showed an increase from December to February.

    B.   Provide the student with extra independent reading practice at home in order to increase reading skills such as comprehension and vocabulary acquisition.

    C.   Conference with the parents and assist them in implementing an at-home practice program.

    D.   Provide the student with reading interventions during the school day to target his specific literacy issues.

120. Given the data, what instructional adjustments would be most appropriate?

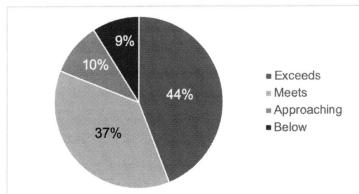

A. Group the students who are approaching and meet grade-level expectations with those who exceed expectations for peer tutoring while providing the students who are struggling with intensive interventions.

B. Send the students who are below grade-level expectations out of the classroom for intensive interventions while delivering whole-group instruction at grade level for the remaining students.

C. Deliver a short, whole-group lesson on a targeted reading standard, then have students rotate through differentiated reading centers while providing appropriate intervention and enrichment at a teacher-led center.

D. Tailor whole-group instruction to meet the needs of those students who meet or exceed grade-level expectations while calling in a resource teacher to work with the other students during the literacy block.

This page intentionally left blank.

Reading | Practice Test Answer Explanations

Number	Answer	Competency	Explanation
1.	B	1	One of the 6 main considerations mentioned in this book when looking over research is relevancy. The research must be relevant for it to be useful. Answers A, C, and D are not considerations needed when looking over research.
2.	B	1	When you think about reliability, think consistency. If a study gets consistent results after multiple trials, the study is reliable.
3.	C	1	Vygotsky and the Zone of Proximal Development are associated with social learning, making answer C the best answer. A KWL activity to activate background knowledge aligns with Piaget and the stages of cognitive development. Whole language is associated with Frank Smith. Finally, silent sustained reading is usually not the correct answer on the exam.
4.	A	1	Internal Validity – The study was conducted properly, and results can be applied *within* the context of the study. External Validity - Results can be generalized to the *outside* world.
5.	D	1	Always associate Piaget with schema or background knowledge. Building schema aligns with Piaget's stages of cognitive development.
6.	A	1	Noam Chomsky believed humans have an instinct or an innate sense of language and literacy. He named this universal grammar, meaning language is basic instinct.
7.	C	1	Constructivism is a holistic philosophy that supports the idea that learning and problem solving should reflect real-life contexts where the environment is rich in information and learning includes authentic tasks.
8.	D	1	In a bottom up approach reading is considered a linear process and the focus should be on phonics. First, the students get the foundations (bottom) of phonics, then they can move onto fluency and comprehension.
9.	B	1	Academic journals contain peer-reviewed research and are the most reliable sources for relevant research.
10.	A	1	The bibliography will contain all the research the author of the study used to conduct his or her research. Look for scholarly research in the study's bibliography to see if the study is appropriate. Be cautious of studies with no bibliography or with a limited bibliography.
11.	D	1	Internal Validity – The student was conducted properly, and results can be applied *within* the context of the study. **External Validity** - Results can be generalized to the *outside* world.
12.	C	1	Louise Rosenblatt theorized that the act of reading literature involves a transaction between the reader and the text. Reading response journals and relating text to self are two activities that align with this theory.

Number	Answer	Competency	Explanation
13.	B	2	This passage presents a main idea, hippos are aggressive, and then gives specific details of the aggression—attacking villagers, 150 attacks in the last 2 years. While this is a problem, no solution is presented, eliminating answer D. Causes and effects were not discussed, eliminating answer choice A. Finally, this passage is not in chronological order.
14.	D	2	In this example, the author has unlimited knowledge of the thoughts and actions of both characters, Jade and Sarah. Therefore, this is written in third-person omniscient. Omniscient means all-knowing.
15.	D	2	Using a balanced literacy program in class, using both literary and informational text, is the best answer here. All the answer choices are ok activities. However, answer D has all the good words to look for in an answer choice for Competency 2.
16.	A	2	**Autobiographies** – Text that describes one's own life. The author is the person in the autobiography. **Biographies** – Text that tells the life of another person. The author is not the person in the biography. **Historical fiction** – Fictional stories set during a real event or time in history. These stories will have historically accurate events and locations. **Expository Nonfiction** – Text that informs the reader. The author is objective.
17.	C	2	The most important question out of all 4 listed is answer C. It is important to show diverse characters not in stereotypical roles, but rather in powerful dynamic roles, so students from diverse backgrounds can see themselves in the stories.
18.	C	2	When choosing multicultural text, considering the presentation of issues means the teacher is considering the accuracy of the topics presented. For example, in a book about slavery, the teacher should make sure there are not details left out. In addition, the text should be appropriate for the grade level.
19.	C	2	The first thing to consider when planning a lesson or choosing materials is the state-adopted standards.
20.	A	2	The measures the teacher is using, observations, are qualitative. They cannot be quantified, eliminating answer B and C. Finally, rubric does not fit here.
21.	C	2	Struggling students should use text on their level. They can supplement with above level text, but their main reading should be on their level.
22.	A	2	Different genres include fiction, non-fiction, poetry, folklore, and dramas. Exposing students to all these genres can be achieved by using a classroom library. The other answer choices are specific to only one genre.
23.	A	2	A Haiku is poem consisting of 3 lines and 17 syllables. Each line has a set number of syllables: line 1 has 5 syllables; line 2 has 7 syllables; line 3 has 5 syllables

Number	Answer	Competency	Explanation
24.	B	2	A Lexile level is a complexity measure ranging from BR (Beginning Reader) to 1385. Teachers use Lexile levels to choose appropriate text.
25.	D	3	**Diagnostic** – determine what prior knowledge, preconceptions, or misconceptions students have before starting a lesson. **Norm-reference** – compare students **Formative** – monitor progress **Performance-based** – measure skills application *All are used to make instructional decisions.
26.	D	3	**Criterion-referenced** exams assess a set of standards or criteria. These are state tests. **Formative** – ongoing, informal assessments to monitor progress. **Performance-based** – students apply their skills by performing a task—lab, presentation, etc. **Norm-referenced** – comparing students using a percentile ranking
27.	A	3	Answer choice A has all the good words you should look for in an answer choice about assessment. The correct assessment is being used for the correct measure—diagnostic to measure base-line skills, formative to continuously monitor students' skills. In addition, answer A mentions *data-driven decision making*, which is the most effective approach when using assessments.
28.	C	3	**Summative** – measure the sum or the outcomes of learning. **Norm-reference** – compare students **Diagnostic** – measure preconceptions and misconceptions at the beginning of the lesson **Formative** – monitor progress
29.	B	3	The most effective way to measure students' skills in sequence is to give an oral assessment. Have students verbally explain the events in the story in order. All the other answer choices are either impractical or ineffective.
30.	A	3	The language in answer choice A is in the test specification for this competency. Teachers must use a variety of formal and informal assessments to make clear and effective decisions in the classroom. Answer choice B mentions rewards, which makes it incorrect. Teachers should use more than just performance-based assessments, eliminating answer C. Answer choice D only mentions two formal assessments.

Number	Answer	Competency	Explanation
31.	A	3	Conducting a research project over a long-period of time is a performance-based assessment. The most effective assessment tool for a performance-based assessment is a rubric. A rubric sets the criteria and expectations for the task. Students can reference the rubric as they complete the task to make sure they include everything outlined in the rubric. Finally, teachers use the rubric to score and provide feedback to students.
32.	C	3	A running record is a way to assess students' oral fluency. These assessments are administered differently depending on what the teacher is trying to measure. However, the basic structure is a student reads from a passage. The teacher has a copy of the same passage. The teacher follows along as the student reads. The teacher marks any errors or miscues the student makes during the reading.
33.	D	3	An informal reading inventory (IRI) is an individually administered formative assessment designed to measure student comprehension. This is considered a formative assessment.
34.	B	3	Data-driven decision making is a recurring theme on the FTCE Reading K-12 exam. If you see it in an answer choice, it is definitely the correct answer.
35.	B	3	A level 3 on the Florida Standards Assessment is considered proficient or on grade level. However, students at this level do need additional support to maintain proficiency. Answer choice A is appropriate for a student who scored a level 1 or 2. Answer C and D are not appropriate.
36.	C	3	One way to assess students' reading levels is to calculate how many words per min the students read. There are benchmark levels of how many words per min students should read and at what grade level. None of the other answer choices will assess students' reading levels.
37.	A	4	A main component of intrinsic motivation is competence—feeling equipped to meet the teacher's expectation. Answer A allows students to work on their competence in a safe environment. The other answer choices are ok techniques, but answer A is the most effective.
38.	D	4	Because only 5 students missed the skill, the teacher should only intervene for these students. Therefore, we can eliminate answer choice A and B. A temporary homogeneous group to apply interventions to help these students is best. Using peer-tutors is not the best strategy when students need interventions. The teacher should provide interventions.
39.	B	4	QAR stands for Question Answer Relationships. QAR is an approach to reading comprehension where students generate reading questions. The QAR highlights 4 main question types: right there, think and search, author and you, on my own.

Number	Answer	Competency	Explanation
40.	B	4	The phrase *information rich* is in the test specifications for this competency. Therefore, we can consider answer B as the best choice.
41.	C	4	Goal setting in an intrinsic motivator. In addition, this answer contains good words—data, goals. All the other answer choices are extrinsic motivators.
42.	A	4	The teacher is thinking about students learning preferences, also known as multiple intelligences—brochure (visual), podcast (auditory), performance (kinesthetic), and an essay (read/write).
43.	A	4	The most effective way to help students is by making data-driven decisions. Answer choice A outlines data driven decisions. Answer B is incorrect because you never want to keep students in homogeneous groups. Homogeneous groups should be used temporarily to provide interventions. Grouping by behavior is ineffective for this task. Grouping by interest will not necessarily help students.
44.	D	4	Speaking and listening are key words in the question. Role play is the only activity listed that includes speaking and listening.
45.	B	4	When answering questions on the FTCE Reading K-12 Test, repeated reading is a good answer for struggling reader questions. Using Basal Reading to read and then reread helps to reinforce students' skills.
46.	C	4	According to self-determination theory, intrinsic motivation is driven by three things: autonomy, relatedness, and competence.
47.	C	4	Practicing procedures so students know exactly how to move efficiently through flexible grouping is the best answer here. This is a classroom management question related to the reading classroom.
48.	D	4	Relatedness is an intrinsic motivator and the best answer here.
49.	A	5	Because no letters or words are used and students are using the picture to say the word frog, the students are in the pre-alphabetic stage (before letter stage).
50.	B	5	Morphology is the study of words, specifically the smallest units of meanings in words. Morphemes are units of meaning in words. Phonemes are the smallest units of sound in words. Semantics is the overall meaning in words and sentences, not individual meanings. Phonics aligns with spelling.
51.	A	5	Discourse means speech or dialogue which is most appropriate for speaking and listening.
52.	C	5	Morphology is the study of the smallest meanings in words. Prefixes, suffixes, and roots affect the meanings in words. For example, in the word *unbelievable*, the prefix is a unit of meaning (not).
53.	D	5	Phonological awareness is an overarching skill that includes identifying and manipulating units of oral language, including parts of words, syllables, onsets, and rimes.

Number	Answer	Competency	Explanation
54.	D	5	Semantics is a cuing system that uses meaning. You can remember this as the *m* in se*m*antics as *meaning*.
55.	C	5	Phonemic awareness focuses on the sounds in words. Therefore, this activity will be mostly auditory.
56.	C	5	Phonics focuses on the rules for symbols in words. For example, a vowel in a word is long when it is followed by another vowel, or when it is followed by a consonant and then a vowel. Those rules make up phonics. Answer choice A is usually never the answer on any FTCE. Answer choice B is an activity for high frequency words. Answer choice D describes a phonemic awareness activity.
57.	B	5	This word is broken up by each individual sound in the word. Therefore, the answer is phonemes. Because each letter is segmented, this word is not broken up by morphemes (prefixes, suffixes or roots), or syllables. Semantics are the meanings of words, which is not appropriate here.
58.	B	5	Because there is the beginning letter of the word ball and a picture of the ball, the students are in the partial alphabetic phase.
59.	D	5	Consolidate means to combine. Students who combine their skills in phonemic awareness, phonics, phonological awareness are in the consolidated alphabetic stage.
60.	D	5	Syntax focuses on the structure of words. The cognitive working system described in the question is a syntactic cuing system
61.	B	5	Morphology is associated with the study of prefixes suffixes and roots in words. Therefore, the best use of words for a morphology lesson is answer choice B.
62.	B	6	In this activity, the students are using onset and rime. Onsets are the beginning consonant and consonant cluster; in this case tr is the onset. Rime is the vowel and consonants that follow. Some common rimes are: -ack, -an, -aw, -ick, -ing, -op, -unk, -ain, -ank, -ay, -ide, -ink, -or, -ock, -ight, -ame, -eat, -ine.
63.	A	6	The key words in the question stem *is instead of*. That indicates the teacher and students are replacing or substituting one sound for another in a word. Substitution is a phonemic awareness activity.
64.	A	6	Working with individual sounds in words is phonemic awareness. Answers B, C, and D all focus on phonics, which means students have to see the words and apply spelling rules. That is not what's happening in the activities listed.
65.	D	6	High frequency words are sight words. They should be memorized because they occur all the time in text.
66.	C	6	CVCC is consonant, vowel, consonant, consonant. The only answer choices that follows that pattern is answer C—*tack*.

Number	Answer	Competency	Explanation
67.	C	6	Use process of elimination for this question. The students are in the emergent stage or the very beginning stage of reading. Literature circles in answer A and working with stories and writing in D are both high level activities. These are not activities for the emergent stage of reading; eliminate choices A and D. Answer C is better than answer B because decoding skills require phonics knowledge. In addition, oral language (answer C) is the first skill students acquire. Therefore, answer C is the best choice.
68.	D	6	The silent letter combinations is a phonics issue. Students have to understand that when they see a *kn*, *wr* or *gn*, that the initial consonant is silent. This is a phonics exercise.
69.	B	6	Clapping syllables in words is an effective strategy for syllable instruction in the early primary grades. Answers C and D are ineffective. Decoding is used for phonics and reading. Clapping is most appropriate for this question.
70.	A	6	In both cases the students delete the initial consonant sound. Therefore, deletion is the answer.
71.	B	6	Sight words should be memorized. A memorization game is most appropriate.
72.	C	6	Even if you didn't know that what a digraph or a vowel team is, the instructional approach should cue you to choose small group. Only a few students are struggling; therefore, small-group is most appropriate. Also, *ou* is two vowels; vowel teams is most appropriate.
73.	D	6	Consonant blends include two or three graphemes blended together. You may be tempted to choose answer A because there are two consonants together in those words. However, those are not blends; they are considered doublets.
74.	D	6	In the word receive, the /c/ makes an /s/ sound because of the phonics rule *i* before e except after *c*.
75.	C	6	Morphemes are the smallest units of meaning in words. In addition, focusing on compound words is a lesson in morphology.
76.	C	7	When teaching vocabulary, students must have the opportunity to interact with words in an authentic manner. Answer A is a best practice because using context clues allows the students to figure out new vocabulary by evaluating words and ideas around the vocabulary words. Answer B is also a best practice because analyzing prefixes, suffixes, and roots is a way to deconstruct a word by understanding its word parts. Answer D is also a best practice because word walls are interactive. Out of all the answers, answer C is not the best practice. Dictionaries are amazing tools to use as a supplement to instruction. However, explicitly using a dictionary is not an authentic practice in vocabulary instruction
77.	A	7	Listen vocabulary is the first step in vocabulary acquisition. Therefore, the teacher should focus on this stage.

Number	Answer	Competency	Explanation
78.	D	7	Tier I words are used in everyday speech. These words are learned in conversation. They rarely require direct instruction. These words are often referred to as sight words. Examples: see, happy, what
79.	D	7	On the FTCE Reading K-12 Test, using context clues is considered the best choice for vocabulary. When words are difficult, having students understand them in context is most effective.
80.	A	7	The key word here is *conversational*. That lends itself to a role play activity. In addition, role play helps students to use vocabulary in the real world, which is always effective in vocabulary instruction.
81.	C	7	Remember, context is considered a good word on this exam. Contextual analysis is using context.
82.	A	7	Tier II words are words that occur across contexts. More common in writing and everyday speech, these words enhance comprehension of a text. These words are best used for targeted explicit vocabulary instruction. Answer A is the best choice.
83.	D	7	Tier III words are low frequency words. They are limited to a specific domain. They often pertain to a specific content area. They are best learned within the content of the lesson or subject matter. Examples: molecule, mitochondria
84.	D	7	The two skills students use to express ideas is speaking and writing. Reading and listening are receptive skills.
85.	B	7	Receptive vocabulary includes reading and listening skills. The only activity where students are using receptive vocabulary is listening to a story on tape. All the other answer choices work on expressive vocabulary.
86.	C	7	Expressive vocabulary includes speaking and writing skills. The only activity where students are using expressive vocabulary is discussion. All the other answer choices work on receptive vocabulary.
87.	B	7	In this case, *she* and *place* are sight words. They are high-frequency, tier I words. *Lithosphere* is a tier III word because it is specific to a content area like science. *Examined* is tier II word. It is not a sight word and is not an academic-specific word.
88.	C	7	This is academic vocabulary that is specific to a content area (biology). Therefore, these are tier III words.
89.	B	7	Context is a good word on this exam. In addition, it makes the most sense when a student is reading. All the other answer choices break up the reading. Context clues will most likely be the correct answer if you see it in an answer choice in a question about vocabulary.

Number	Answer	Competency	Explanation
90.	B	8	Fluency is important because it reduces cognitive energy needed to decode words. Students can then apply that cognitive energy to understanding the text. Fluency frees up the brain to work on more complex tasks, like predicting, questioning, and evaluating—all essential skills in comprehension.
91.	B	8	Prosody is reading with expression while using the words and punctuation correctly. Reading with prosody means the reader is conveying what is on the page, pausing at commas and periods, and using inflection based on punctuation.
92.	D	8	If the student is stopping when encountering high-frequency words (sight words) to decode them, the student is struggling with fluency. Having automaticity when reading is essential in the comprehension process. Automaticity reduces the cognitive demand needed for decoding. That reduced cognitive demand can then be applied to the comprehension process. Focusing on spelling (answer A) is not the best approach. A diagnostic test (answer B) is unnecessary because the teacher can already see the problem is fluency. Answer C is not the best choice because it is essentially repeating what the teacher can already see: the student is having trouble with fluency.
93.	B	8	Predicting is a high-level skill and coincides with comprehension. Students cannot predict what is going to happen unless they have an understanding of the text's meaning. Fluency and decoding are skills used in the emergent stage of reading. Predication is used in the later stages of reading. Automaticity has to do with fluency. Comprehension involves making predictions and asking questions.
94.	D	8	Comprehension is the goal. Therefore, answer D is the best choice. When answering questions about reading, look for those "good" words. Answer D has words like complex text and comprehend.
95.	C	8	This is a timed fluency read. Timing has to do with rate. Tallying miscues has to do with accuracy.
96.	D	8	Prosody is reading with expression while using the words and punctuation correctly. Reading with prosody means the reader is conveying what is on the page, pausing at commas and periods and using inflection based on punctuation. Prosody and fluency are related skills. All the other answer choices have to do with comprehension.
97.	A	8	This is a critical thinking question. Notice answer A has the word analyze. Competency 8 focuses on comprehension and critical thinking. Be sure to look for the verbs that align with critical thinking.
98.	A	8	The key words in this question are *think and listen critically.* The word *critically* indicates a high-level function. Therefore, we should look for the answer that has the high-level Bloom's Taxonomy words; in this case, Answer A contains the verb *evaluate.*

Number	Answer	Competency	Explanation
99.	A	8	The key word here is *evaluating.* *Evaluate* and *critical thinking* always go together.
100.	C	8	Answer choice C has all the good words in it—*differentiated, targeted interventions.* Comprehension games and partner reads are not as effective as differentiated instruction. Because there is a group of students struggling, whole group is not the best choice.
101.	D	8	All of the techniques in the answer choices are beneficial in developing students' literacy across content areas.
102.	C	8	Critical thinking means higher-order skills. Evaluate is at the top of the pyramid for higher order skills.
103.	B	8	Asking questions about the text develops comprehension. Question generation, prediction, and summarization are all comprehension skills.
104.	C	8	Responding to text in a journal would be the most appropriate way to relate text to self. Jigsaw is breaking a text up among cooperative learning partners. Think-pair-share is a group activity. Literature circles is a discussion activity.
105.	A	8	The teacher is modeling her thinking process and showing students how to think about their thinking. This is metacognition.
106.	B	8	Jigsaw is a cooperative learning activity in which each student or groups of students read and analyze a small piece of information that is part of a much larger piece. They then share what they've learned with the class. This is a comprehension activity.
107.	C	8	First, determine what the question is asking: synthesizing reading material. Synthesize is a higher-order skill. Answer choice C has the word brainstorming in it, which alludes to synthesizing. Also, using theme, content, characters, and details is a way to synthesize information. You may be tempted to choose A; however, that activity is concerned with the structure or organizational pattern of the text, which is a different skill from synthesizing. Eliminate answer D because rewriting a play is not going to help with synthesizing. Eliminate B because it is mainly concerned with supporting details of the text.
108.	D	8	Summarizing is focusing on key aspects of the reading.
109.	A	9	Teachers should meet regularly with paraprofessionals to plan instruction and maximize resources for student learning. Also, the only reasonable answer choice is choice A. All the other answer choices are examples of how not to use a paraprofessional.

Number	Answer	Competency	Explanation
110.	D	9	This is a case of using data to determine literacy skills to drive instructional decisions in content area reading. This is a box and whisker plot. Even if you have never seen a chart like this, you should be able to make an educated guess based on the lines and elements presented. The two dashes on the side of each graph are the proficiency bars. Based on that you can see that the students are above proficiency in letter recognition but below proficiency in word recognition.
111.	C	9	In student-led conferences, students go over their data and work with parents/caregivers. The student is in charge of communicating goals and achievements. This is the most effective for this scenario.
112.	B	9	This scenario outlines what action research is. Action research involves analyzing assessment data. Making decisions based on that data, and continuously monitoring progress along the way. Action research is often done in PLCs.
113.	B	9	Formative assessments are informal checks to use as progress monitoring. Therefore, B is the best answer. Scheduling team meetings, as in answer A, is not going to help with informal progress monitoring. Answer C references formal assessments, but the leadership team found that informal progress monitoring is necessary. Hiring additional coaches to track growth does not help to train teachers in informal progress monitoring
114.	A	9	For a whole-group activity, the best place for the paraprofessionals is walking around the room and helping when needed.
115.	C	9	Setting clear expectations and roles is essential. Remember, answer A—rules and regulations—sounds punitive, so eliminate it. Student data is confidential and should not be shared with volunteers. Faculty meeting schedule is unrelated.
116.	D	9	The only thing that will tell a teacher if a program worked is assessment data. Remember, surveys measure attitudes and feelings. They do not measure achievement.
117.	A	9	Answer A is most realistic and helpful in parent involvement scenarios. Answer B and C require too much from the parents. Answer D is punitive.
118.	A	9	The only way to determine if the program was successful in increasing students reading skills is to measure reading outcomes. None of the other answer choices will tell the teacher if the program was effective in increasing reading skills.
119.	D	9	Notice that D has all of the good words—interventions, target—associated with using data to meet the needs of every student.
120.	C	9	Notice all the good words in this answer choice C: reading standard, differentiated, appropriate intervention. Also, because there are a variety of levels in this class, providing students the opportunity to work as a whole and then break out into differentiated reading centers is appropriate.

This page intentionally left blank.

Glossary of Terms

The following is a list of important words organized by competency. Understanding these words will help you identify correct answers on the FTCE Reading K-12 Test.

COMPETENCY 1 VOCABULARY

Validity - how sound the research is in both the design and methods

Reliability - the degree of consistency in the measure

Jean Piaget – associated with KWL chart, schema, stages of cognitive development

Lev Vygotsky – associated with cooperative learning, social learning, zone of proximal development.

Noam Chomsky – associated with the theory that language is innate in humans, universal grammar

Frank Smith – whole language approach

Louis Rosenblatt – reading is a transaction between reader and text, text to self

Constructivism - learning and problem solving should reflect real-life contexts

KWL – graphic organizer that helps activate background knowledge

COMPETENCY 2 VOCABULARY

Multiculturalism – choosing literature that accurately represents people of color, circumstances and culture.

Culturally Responsive – choose literature and classroom methods that celebrate culture and help students seek to engage with and understand different cultures.

Measures of Text Complexity – using several data points—qualitative, quantitative, and reader and task—to determine what text to use in the classroom.

COMPETENCY 3 VOCABULARY

Diagnostic Assessment – pre-assessment that measures preconceptions and misconceptions

Formative Assessment – informal, ongoing, progress monitoring

Criterion-Reference Assessment – state standardized test

Norm-Referenced Assessment – percentile comparison

Running Record – fluency assessment to calculate correct words per min (wpm)

Rubrics – evaluation tool that sets expectations for projects and writing

COMPETENCY 4 VOCABULARY

Homogeneous Groups – everyone is the same level in the group

Heterogeneous Groups – students of different levels in a group

Basal Reading – Dick and Jane series

Shared Reading – students and teacher share in the process of reading

Guided Reading – teacher guides the process of reading

SQ3R – reading strategy that stands for survey, question, read, recite, review

QAR – question answer relationships

Repeated Reading – used to help with fluency and comprehension

Readers Theater – Each student reads a part of the text

Choral Reading – reading aloud unison

Multiple Intelligences – learning preferences (visual, read/write, kinesthetic, auditory)

COMPETENCY 5 and 6 VOCABULARY

Phonological Awareness – all the skills put together in word recognition

Phonemic Awareness – sounds only in words

Phonics – spelling and rules of letters (*ph* makes a /f/ sound)

Cueing Systems – cognitive process for figuring out words in context (semantic, syntactic, graphophonic)

Semantic – using meaning to figure out words in context

Syntactic – using structure to figure out words in context

Graphophonic – using phonics to figure out words in context

Morphology – the study of meaning in words (compound words, prefixes, suffixes and roots)

COMPETENCY 7 VOCABULARY

Sight Words – high frequency words students should memorize

Vocab Acquisition – acquiring listening, speaking, reading, and writing vocabulary in that order

Tier I Vocabulary – sight words (see, how, the, going)

Tier II Vocabulary – harder words that are still in most books (immense, inaccurate, cultural)

Tier III Vocabulary – domain specific (artillery, chromosome, cartilage)

COMPETENCY 8 VOCABULARY

Fluency - the ability to read with speed, accuracy, and proper expression.

Automaticity – reading at >95% accuracy

Prosody – reading with inflection

Rate – correct words per min (wpm)

Accuracy – reading the correct words

Comprehension – higher-order skill used to understand text

Metacognition – thinking about the process of thinking

COMPETENCY 9 VOCABULARY

Stakeholders – anyone with a stake in the school—students, teachers, parents, and community members

Action Research – continuously collecting data and making decisions in the classroom

Data-Driven – using data (qualitative and quantitative) to measure the effectiveness of programs, strategies and approaches in the classroom

Good Words and Phrases

The following list of words contains what we call good words. You will see these words in the correct answer choices on the exam. We know many of you like to make flashcards and memorize important concepts. This list of words is worth remembering and studying. If you see any of these words in an answer choice on the exam, chances are, it's the correct answer.

Accommodations

Modifying instruction or using supports to help ELLs achieve. Accommodations do NOT involve lowering the standard or delaying learning.

Bilingual education

Using elements from the students' L1 to support L2. Just say NO to English only practices.

Celebrate culture

Activities in the classroom that help students learn and observe other cultures.

Classroom management

A variety of skills and techniques that teachers use to keep students organized, orderly, focused, attentive, on task, and academically productive during class.

Communicating data with stakeholders

Stakeholders include students, parents, teachers, administrators, community members, and local business owners. Teachers must organize data and effectively communicate achievement results with all stakeholders.

Critical thinking

Higher-order thinking skills that involve evaluating, analyzing, creating, and applying knowledge.

Cultural responsiveness

Instruction as a pedagogy that empowers students intellectually, socially, and emotionally by celebrating and learning about other cultures.

Data-driven decision making

Using scores, writing samples, observations, and other types of qualitative and quantitative data to make instructional decisions.

Diverse perspectives

Recognizing that students bring with them their perspectives and experiences to the learning environment.

Diversity as an asset

Seeing diversity in the classroom as an opportunity to learn new things through the perspectives of others.

Evidence-based

Using evidence in the form of data or research to make decisions in the classroom.

Follow the IEP

The IEP is a legal document. If you see IEP in the answer choices, it is most likely the answer.

High expectations for ALL students

Holding all students to high academic standards regardless of the students' achievement level, ethnicity, language, socioeconomic status.

Honoring stages of language acquisition

Do not rush students. Let them take their time in language acquisition.

Interactive activities for reading

Seek out activities in content area reading that are interactive and real-world based. Making content reading interesting is key.

Interdisciplinary activities

Activities that connect two or more content areas; promotes relevance and critical thinking.

Interdisciplinary units

A teaching approach that combines the curricular objectives and methods from more than one discipline focusing on a central theme, issue, problem or works.

Intrinsic motivation

Answers that promote autonomy, relatedness, and competence are ways to apply intrinsic motivation. Be on the lookout for these answer choices.

Native/home language

Students' first language, which is often the language students speak in their homes with their parents or guardians.

Outcomes

The results of a program, strategy, or resources implemented in the classroom.

Procedures

Classroom routines that rid students of distractions that waste time and interfere with learning.

Relevance, real-world, and relatable

Be sure to choose answers that promote real-world application and make learning relatable to students' lives.

Research-based

Referencing scholarly research to decide what strategies and programs to use in the classroom.

Rigor

Expectations and experiences that are academically and intellectually challenging.

Safe times to use academic English

Make the classroom a safe space for ELLs to practice L2.

Scaffolding

Using supports to help students achieve a standard that they would not achieve on their own.

State standards

A criterion set by the state that outlines the expected skills students must master for each grade level.

Student centered/learner centered

A wide variety of educational programs, learning experiences, instructional approaches, and academic-support strategies that address the distinct learning needs, interests, or cultural backgrounds of students.

Student interest

Paying attention to what students want to learn about.

Specific and meaningful feedback

More than just a grade at the top of a paper, effective feedback includes positive aspects and how students can apply those positive aspects to improving. In addition, feedback should contain specific things the student should do to improve.

Vocabulary in context

Always teach vocabulary in context. It helps to relate the vocabulary to the real-world.

Bibliography

Agosto, D. E. (2002). *Criteria for evaluating multicultural literature*. Retrieved from http://www.pages. drexel.edu/~dea22/multicultural.html

Chun, M. (2010). Taking teaching to (performance) task: Linking pedagogical and assessment practices. *Change: The Magazine of Higher Education*.

Heggerty, Ed.D., M. (2003). *Phonemic Awareness: The Skills They Need To Help Them Succeed!* https:// wps.prenhall.com/chet_nes_v2bridgedemo_1/185/47611/12188671.cw/content/index.html

Landt, S. M. (2006). Multicultural literature and young adolescents: A kaleidoscope of opportunity. Journal of Adolescent & Adult Literacy, 49(8), 690-697.

Lapp, D., Moss, B., Grant, M., and Johnson, K. (2015). Close look at close reading: teaching students to analyze complex texts, grades K–5. Retrieved from http://www.ascd.org/publications/ books/114008/chapters/Understanding-and-Evaluating-Text-Complexity.aspx

Omaggio, M. A. (1993). *Teaching language in context*. Boston: Heinle and Heinle.

Rasinski, T. & Padak, N. (2005). *3-Minute Reading Assessments*. New York, NY: Scholastic Inc.

Shafer, Greg (1998) "Whole Language: Origins and Practice," Language Arts Journal of Michigan: Vol. 14: Iss. 1, Article 5. Available at: https://doi.org/10.9707/2168-149X.1429

Shioshita, J. (1997). Beyond good intentions: Selecting multicultural literature. *Children's Advocate* newsmagazine.

The International Reading Association (n.d.). *A Critical Analysis of Eight Informal Reading Inventories*. Retrieved from https://www.readingrockets.org/article/critical-analysis-eight-informal-reading-inventories.

University of Massachusetts Boston (2019). Evaluating sources. Retrieved from https://umb.libguides. com/c.php?g=351182&p=2367584

Urbandale Community School District (2019). Instructional materials: Selection, inspection, and reconsideration. Retrieved from http://www.urbandaleschools.com/policy/article-600-educational-program/627-instructional-materials-selection-inspection-and-reconsideration/

Whitehurst, G., & Lonigan, C. (1998). Child Development and Emergent Literacy. *Child Development, 69*(3), 848-872. doi:10.2307/1132208

Willis, S. (1995). Whole language: Finding the surest way to literacy. Curriculum: ACSD. Retrieved from http://www.ascd.org/publications/curriculum-update/fall1995/Whole-Language.aspx

Made in the USA
Columbia, SC
30 October 2020